Charting a COURSE in Your Youth

All Scripture quotations are taken from the
KING JAMES VERSION.

ISBN: 978-1-936208-56-2

Cover design: Kristi Yoder
Layout design: Felicia Kern
Front cover photos: istockphoto.com, map by Gary Miller
Illustrations by Nathan Wright

Third printing: November 2015

For more information about Christian Aid Ministries, see page 209.

Published by:
TGS International
P.O. Box 355
Berlin, Ohio 44610 USA
Phone: 330·893·4828
Fax: 330·893·2305
www.tgsinternational.com

TGS001100

Charting a COURSE *in Your Youth*

A SERIOUS CALL TO EXAMINE YOUR
FAITH, FOCUS, AND FINANCES

Gary Miller

Dedication

TO THE GROWING NUMBER OF VIBRANT BELIEVERS WHO ARE EXHIBITING A PASSION FOR THE KINGDOM IN THEIR YOUTH. YOUR WILLINGNESS TO TURN YOUR BACK ON A GODLESS SOCIETY AND FOCUS ON SERVING THE LORD JESUS HAS BEEN ENCOURAGING.

YOU HAVE INSPIRED ME!

Table of Contents

Introduction

"I am a Christian, and will remain a Christian, and obey only the commandments of Christ all the days of my life."[1]

The crowd stared in awe. What kind of stupidity was this? How could this young man calmly respond like this to an angry king? The king's patience was gone, and he was obviously ready to use torture if the young man did not obey. Kings were not used to being trifled with. Yet each time this young man was given a command that conflicted with his convictions, he responded in the same way: "I am a Christian."

The day had started out so nicely. The king wanted to give him a second chance. Pelagius was intelligent and handsome. He had a lot going for him, and the king assumed he could be persuaded to give up this faith in Jesus Christ. So the king called Pelagius in and promised him pleasure if he would just renounce his faith.

"Just imagine living right here in the royal court," said the king. "If you are willing to renounce this Jesus Christ, you will have the best the kingdom has to offer.

"In fact," the king continued, "I want you to imagine your greatest fantasy. Picture the greatest pleasure you can imagine. Whatever it is, it will be yours if you will only renounce this Christianity."

But Pelagius stood firm. He was willing to turn his back on the best his culture had to offer. The king, seeing that the promise of worldly wealth and pleasure was not enough to shake this man's faith in Christ, tried torture. Pelagius was suspended in the air for over six hours and cruelly tormented. His persecutors continued to offer him relief and freedom if he would only renounce his Lord. But Pelagius valiantly continued to affirm his faith in Jesus Christ.

Finally, in exasperation, the king commanded that Pelagius be brought before him. Furious, he ordered that Pelagius's limbs be removed. As Pelagius stood before the king, dripping with blood from his previous tortures, he prayed aloud to his God, saying, "O Lord, deliver me out of the hands of my enemies." As he lifted his hands in prayer, the executioners pulled them apart and cut off first one arm, and then the other. After this they cut off his legs, and finally his head. It was June 29, 925 A.D., and Pelagius remained faithful unto death.[a]

It took incredible faith and commitment for men like Pelagius to remain faithful. But something made this particular persecution different from many others. Pelagius was only thirteen years old. He hadn't had many years to prepare for this final hour of testing, trial, and temptation. He wasn't a seasoned old saint who could draw from years of experience and memories of God's faithfulness. But history records that he had used his time wisely, reading the Scriptures and focusing on the Kingdom of God.

> YOUR MOST DIFFICULT DECISION MIGHT OCCUR IN A DEPARTMENT STORE . . . ON A CAR LOT . . . IN THE SPORTING GOODS STORE OR SHOPPING MALL.

You may never stand face to face with an angry king. You may never have to stand in the midst of a jeering crowd and decide between Jesus and saving your limbs. But you are called to make a choice.

Pelagius faced his decision in the throne room of a frustrated king. Your most difficult decision may take place somewhere else. It might occur in a department store as you weigh which kingdom you want to be identified with. It might happen on a car lot as you wrestle with your need for transportation versus your in-

[a]Author's note: There is controversy regarding the authenticity of the details in this account.

ner craving for acceptance, or in the sporting goods store or shopping mall. Your strongest conflict may take place on the battlefield of technology. Perhaps your strongest temptation is having that new phone or computer. As a new device comes out, suddenly the one you purchased just a few months ago seems inferior. This new one is smaller, faster, and has many more features. Peer pressure is strong in all of these areas, and all of us are affected. A battle is inevitable.

We live in a time of great deception. Satan is unleashing every weapon at his disposal, and he knows his time is short. But God has not left us without warning. His Word warns us what the end of time will be like. The Apostle Paul, writing to Timothy, describes it. Reading over Paul's description is like reading the daily newspaper. He describes the men of that time as covetous, or never satisfied with what they have. Paul says they will be lovers of their own selves. They will be unthankful and lovers of pleasure more than lovers of God.[b] If you were to write a description of the age we live in, could you describe it better than Paul did? While pleasure-seeking has always been a human tendency, today's youth are seeing an extreme push toward self-indulgence. "If it feels good, do it" seems to be the cry of the age.

But God is calling us to renounce the world's pressure to conform and instead to live holy lives separated unto Him. So how are we to do this in our age? Is God's Word still relevant in a time when technology and science continue to dazzle us with new advances? Does the Bible really have pertinent answers to the questions of our day?

Sometimes it seems life was simpler back in the days of Pelagius. The fight was between good and evil, right and wrong. As we read accounts from those earlier days, the battle lines seem clearer. Life was more black and white. But today, gray seems to be the color of choice. No one is sure about anything, and each person claims a right to his own opinion. People reject the thought of absolutes, and truth seems elusive. Telling people in our society that Jesus Christ is the only way or declaring that the Bible is better than other religious books sounds narrow-minded, prejudiced, and intolerant. It is the age of gray.

So how are we to respond to the pressures of this age? How will you

---

[b] 2 Timothy 3:1-5

respond? What will you use as a point of reference, and how will you chart a course through this confusing swirl of ambiguous, shadowy gray?

I believe we can find the answer to these questions in the words of Jesus Himself. People came to Him one time with some questions. They were confused and needed direction, and Jesus gave them this simple formula: "I am the light of the world: he that followeth me shall not walk in darkness, but shall have the light of life."[a]

Follow Me

The solution to gathering darkness is increasing light. Jesus said the light of life is available to the man or woman who follows Him. As we look at how to regard and manage finances and possessions in our lives, we want to begin here—following Jesus. What would our lives look like if we really chose to follow Him? For Pelagius, it meant torture and death. What would be the result of total surrender in your life?

I don't know where you are in your Christian walk. I don't know how Satan tempts you or how strongly material things grip your heart. But I want to encourage you to follow Jesus regardless of the cost. Let His example be the pattern for your life. Be willing to apply the words of Jesus as you make decisions and chart your course.

Being young is exhilarating! There are so many choices, life is exciting, and the possibilities seem endless. But my prayer for your generation is that you will use these amazing opportunities and resources for the Kingdom—that you will faithfully and unashamedly let the light of His Gospel flow through your lives and lips in the midst of a darkening, evil world.

[a]John 8:12

Flying Free | 1

BUT SEEK YE FIRST THE KINGDOM OF GOD,
AND HIS RIGHTEOUSNESS; AND ALL THESE THINGS
SHALL BE ADDED UNTO YOU.
MATTHEW 6:33

I had waited a long time for this moment. I had anticipated it, visualized it, and now the time had come. With a mixture of fear and excitement, I pushed the throttle forward, and the small plane began to roll down the runway. As the plane picked up speed, I slowly pulled back on the yoke, and the little Cessna rattled, shook, and lifted off the runway. I was in the air!

This was not the first time I had rolled down this runway. It wasn't the first time I had heard the roar, pulled back on the yoke, and watched the ground drop away. But this time something was different—I was alone. Always before there had been an instructor sitting beside me. He had told me when to level off, suggested when to turn, and helped me respond as situations unfolded. He had always been there to remind me to lower the flaps or increase my speed. But today I was on my own. There was no one to tell me what to do. I was free!

The Thrill of Freedom

There is nothing in a young person's life quite like the feeling of freedom. As I gained altitude that day, all the apprehension I had felt while hurtling down the runway was gone. All the fears and what-ifs vaporized. I was flying, and I was free. Years later I can still remember that initial intoxicating feeling of freedom. I was the pilot. I would decide how high to go. I would choose which direction to fly and how far to travel. I was in control, and life was good. I sang at the top of my lungs as I continued to gain altitude. It was great! I gave little thought to where I was going. I was flying!

I glanced casually out my window, and my song abruptly died. The barns and houses were much smaller than I had anticipated. In my euphoria I had climbed higher and gone farther than I had planned. I suddenly realized that getting lost was a real possibility. I could just see the morning headlines: "Young pilot gets lost on first solo flight"!

Turning the craft around, I desperately scanned the ground for some landmark to identify my location. This wasn't fun anymore. All the fields below looked the same. I had been told to take off, circle the airport, and land the plane. My original goal had been to do this without smashing anything. But in the excitement of flying on my own, I had forgotten my original goal. Now as I gazed at the array of gauges on the instrument panel, I was painfully aware of my inadequacies as a pilot. I barely knew how to fly a plane, let alone pinpoint my location using instruments. As I feverishly scanned the horizon for the airstrip, I suddenly longed for my instructor. How comforting it would be to ask him what to do and let him give me some direction.

I really hadn't traveled as far from the airport as I had feared, and I was soon circling the runway and preparing to land. My instructor had given me many details that had seemed unimportant at the time. I just wanted to fly, and he fussed around with little things like keeping the proper RPM, watching the airspeed, and setting the flaps to the right degree. It seemed he was constantly nagging about little things like carburetor heat and exact elevation when turning on final approach.

But as I approached the airport, all those seemingly unimportant instructions came to life. My instructor was not with me, but his directives kept surfacing in my mind. If I was going to get this plane and myself on the ground in one piece, I needed to remember every instruction he had tried to pound into me.

I landed safely that day. In my little ten-minute flight I had experienced extreme emotions, from fear and apprehension to excitement and a great sense of accomplishment. That day I learned more than just how to fly solo. I learned some basic life lessons.

The Desire to Fly Free

In our youth we all experience times of wanting to be free. We are held back by school teachers, church leaders, and parents. We are not allowed to do this or say that. We are not supposed to go to this place or wear that particular thing. We grow up surrounded by lists of rules, regulations, and restrictions. But for some bizarre reason, the things we are told not to do seem the most appealing. Why aren't there rules against broccoli and Brussels sprouts? Why don't we have regulations requiring more recreation and less work?

> "WHY AREN'T THERE RULES AGAINST BROCCOLI AND BRUSSELS SPROUTS?"

But no, we grow up being told not to do the very things our flesh cries out for, and we long to leave this rigid, structured environment and fly on our own. Something within us craves the freedom to go where we want and do as we please. We feel like a kite on the end of a string. It's fun to fly, but it would be much more enjoyable, we imagine, if we could just get loose from that string.

Anyone Can Take Off

But aviation instructors understand something young pilots forget. It's not hard to get a plane off the runway. In fact, anyone who can drive a car can get a plane in the air. Just point the nose of the plane down the runway, give it some power, and pull back on the yoke. It's easy. But taking off is just the beginning. There is much more to flying than just getting off the ground, and the same is true in life. It is not hard to start making your own decisions; the difficulty is in making good ones that hold you to your course and land you safely at your destination.

You may have grown up listening to teaching on money and its proper uses. Perhaps you have been told not to spend too much on this, or the importance of saving for that. Maybe your parents remind you not to waste money on things of no value, and you grow weary of the constant reminders. Perhaps, even now, you long to be liberated from continual cautions and warnings. Maybe you just long to be free.

Trust Godly Instructors

Proverbs says, "The fear of the LORD is the beginning of knowledge: but fools despise wisdom and instruction."[a] This means that a wise young man or woman will value instruction. I encourage you to appreciate godly teachers. Instructors see things differently. They tend to look beyond the thrill of the moment. While I couldn't wait to get that plane in the air, my instructor was more concerned that I was prepared to get the plane back on the ground. Your relationship with those in authority is similar. While you may long to fly free, they are more concerned about where you will eventually end up. Most of us in our youth are not prepared for the challenges ahead.

Box Canyons

Just off the south end of the runway at Lake Tahoe Airport in California is a canyon. The airport is high in elevation, which means the air is thinner and it can be difficult for a small plane to gain altitude in warm weather. The south end of the airport is surrounded by mountains, so there are not many options for a pilot who is having difficulty gaining altitude while departing toward the south.

To those unfamiliar with the local terrain, this canyon looks like the perfect solution. It looks like a great place to fly into while gaining enough altitude to clear the surrounding mountains. But the locals know this canyon provides false hope. It is a box canyon. In other words, once you get into it, there is no way out. The abundance of aluminum hanging from trees at the end of the canyon tells the story of many pilots who flew in and never came back. The apparent solution is an illusion.

The Illusion of Materialism

Satan offers many box canyons today, and he would love to have you fly into one. His desire is to persuade you to trust in what is seen—to simply believe that happiness, peace, and fulfillment come from the things around you, and that more possessions will satisfy your inner longings. Satan would love to convince you to focus on

[a]Proverbs 1:7

accumulating more of this world's goods and living for today. But one of the purposes of this book is to reveal that this enticement is nothing more than a box canyon. Life can be discouraging. Disappointments come. Friends let us down. At times it seems there is no way out.

We try to rise above the discouragement. We try to gain altitude. And Satan will place the temptation of possessions right in our path. It looks so good and seems like the perfect solution. If I just had one of those, then I would be appreciated. Life would be better if I had more of that. If I could just get a nicer car or more stylish clothes, then I would feel accepted by my friends. But materialism is a box canyon. Many fly in and never return.

Fly Higher!

Jesus calls you to rise above this illusion. Everything you own, everything you see, everything you touch—absolutely everything that surrounds you today—will soon be gone. Jesus asks you to turn your back on the things that are seen and put your trust in Him. He offers eternal blessing and joy unspeakable to the young person who, like Pelagius, ignores the offerings of this world and follows Him.

Conclusion

All of us are eventually turned loose. Our parents climb out of the cockpit and we are free to go. We make the decisions. It is wonderful to have our own checkbooks, debit cards, and cash with no one to tell us how to use them. The possibilities seem endless.

An amazing array of options exists for young people today, and our world tells us we can have it all. Fun and excitement are advertised on every corner, and if you don't mind a little debt, you can experience it all now. But remember, there are also many box canyons. A prepared pilot is aware that the canyon just off the runway at Lake Tahoe is deadly. When he sees the canyon ahead after takeoff, he does not see a solution—he sees potential destruction. He has studied the map and listened to his instructor, and he is ready.

As we proceed, let's open our hearts to the truth of God's Word concerning money and possessions. Let's allow His Spirit and Word to be the map and instructor in our lives. God sees life from a higher level, and He is greatly concerned. He is fully aware of the potential hazards that threaten to destroy us. Seeing things from God's perspective will cause you to see things differently.

For Further Reflection

1. What are some box canyons that Satan tempts young people with today?

2. Share examples of times you have been lured into a materialistic trap. What were the consequences?

3. Do you find yourself more susceptible to these temptations in certain situations or moods? If so, what conditions make temptations more intense?

4. How have you overcome or avoided one of these traps?

The Importance of Vision | 2

THE MOST PATHETIC PERSON IN THE WORLD IS SOMEONE WHO HAS SIGHT, BUT HAS NO VISION.
—HELEN KELLER

Sonya Carson returned home from work to disheartening news. As a single mom in Detroit's inner city, she already carried a heavy load. Her husband had walked out on her several years earlier, leaving her to support their two sons. Sonya held two and sometimes even three jobs to stay ahead of the bills. Days were long and work hard to find. Racial prejudice ran high in the 1950s, so a black woman with only a third-grade education found it almost impossible to get a job. When Sonya finally did find someone willing to give her work, the wages were always extremely low.

On this day she returned home to discover that both of her sons were failing in school. Her youngest son, Benjamin, was at the bottom of his class, and his classmates called him a dummy to his face.

Sonya desperately wanted her sons to receive a better education than she had, and the school report was like a kick in the stomach. She wanted her boys to be able to provide for their own families and become productive members of their communities. She wanted them to succeed where she had failed. But this did not seem likely. The neighborhood she lived in did not provide much encouragement. There were few role models for her boys. Indeed, most children growing up in this neighborhood had little hope of productive lives. They spent their time sitting in front of televisions or roaming the streets painting graffiti on walls and looking for mischief.

What could Sonya do? How could she break the endless cycle of welfare, crime, alcohol, gangs, and unemployment that surrounded her? She couldn't teach her sons. She didn't even know how to read.

She had good reason to be concerned; the odds were totally against her. The chances of her boys ever becoming anything other than welfare recipients or prisoners were extremely slim.

But Sonya had one weapon, and she used it against the insurmountable odds she faced that day. She had a vision!

Sonya's Vision

Sonya was able to look beyond the discouragement of the moment. She saw further than the neighborhood surrounding her. Sonya saw her sons' potential. She knew education was critical, and she was determined to follow her vision.

Sonya set about to reverse the discouraging downward spiral. From that day on, when the boys came home from school, they were required to stay inside until their homework was completed. In addition, she required them to read two books from the public library each week. Then, though she couldn't read what they had written, she asked them to write reports on what they had read.

Within a few weeks, change was evident. Benjamin astonished his classmates by identifying rock samples his teacher brought to class, recognizing the rocks from one of the books he had read. "At that moment I realized I wasn't stupid," he recalled later. Curtis, too, began to excel in school.

Benjamin continued to amaze his classmates with his newfound passion for knowledge, and in just one year he went from the bottom of his fifth-grade class to the top of his sixth-grade class.

A Contagious Vision

But knowledge was not the only thing Sonya's boys were gaining. Their mother's determination was contagious. A hunger for more knowledge took hold of them. With their excellent grades, Curtis became an engineer, and Benjamin was accepted at Yale and then went on to medical school at the University of Michigan. After graduating with a degree in neurosurgery, he began practicing at Johns Hopkins University. At only thirty-two years of age he became the director of pediatrics and was one of the most famous and gifted surgeons in the world. Starting in the 1980s, his surgeries to separate Siamese twins made international headlines, and his pioneering techniques revolutionized the field of neurosurgery.

Rising out of a hopeless situation in the slums of Detroit, Ben Carson has become a symbol of hope to many African-Americans who still live in these settings. Books have been written about his life, a movie has been made about him, and he was even lauded in the White House, where he received the Medal of Freedom. His mother may not have had much money or education, but she had vision. And that burning vision, accompanied by her determination to follow it, was powerful enough to propel her sons out of a hopeless situation.

A Driving Vision

The importance of vision in our lives cannot be overemphasized. It becomes the driving force that motivates our actions and sets our course. Think about famous inventors. Many of them attempted things that looked totally unattainable to others. Though ridiculed, they pressed on. They carried in their minds a mental picture that fueled their determination.

The vision of a practical and useful light bulb kept Thomas Edison going. Day after day he pursued his dream. He ignored the thousands of failures in his search for the perfect filament. Catching only snatches of sleep in pursuit of his goal, Edison pressed on until he succeeded.

Or think about the massive immigration during the gold rush. Vision inspired hundreds of thousands of immigrants to leave their homes and follow the Oregon Trail in the 1840s and 1850s. Those early settlers had a vision so powerful they were willing to walk away from family, friends, and every-

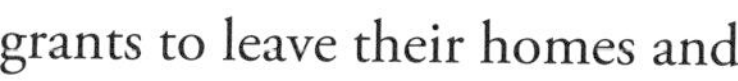

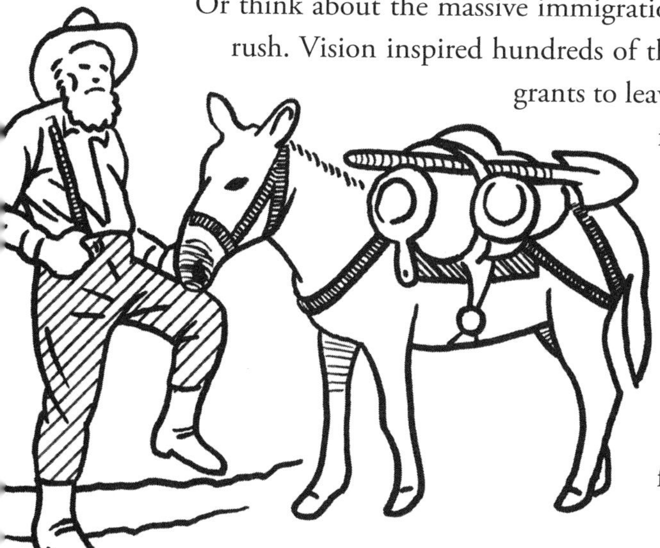

thing they owned.

Vision can be extremely inspiring. But not every vision is good or godly. While some headed west in search of better farmland and a place to raise their families, many were driven by greed. Thousands of men, hearing of gold in California, left their farms, deserted their families, and abandoned their businesses to pursue the foolish vision of easy money.

> VISION IS A POWERFUL MOTIVATOR. IT DRIVES EVERY PART OF YOUR LIFE.

Vision is a powerful motivator. It drives every part of your life. Stop for a moment and analyze your life. What is your vision? What goals are influencing the decisions you make? These questions are of extreme importance. The goals you develop while you are young will influence and direct your whole life, your work in the Kingdom, and ultimately your eternal destiny.

What Is My Vision?

It can be difficult to discern your vision. It is easy to have godly goals when sitting in a study group or having a discussion with other young people. Someone asks what our vision is, and we know the correct answer: living for the Kingdom of Jesus Christ. That's easy. But is that really your vision? Let's probe just a little. It's not always easy to know your own heart. But take some time to look at a few questions and analyze what is driving your life.

- If someone were to give you one thousand dollars right now, what would you do with it? Your immediate reaction may reveal something about your vision. For example, if your first thought was to help someone who is having a financial hardship, then helping others is a part of your vision. But if your thoughts immediately went to clothing, new technology, or some item you want, your answer reveals something else.

- If you were suddenly given a week to do anything you want, what would you choose? Let your imagination go. What do you really enjoy doing? Again, your answer will reveal something about your vision. How you spend free time tells a lot about your heart.

- Do you spend more time reading the Bible and godly writings than newspapers, magazines, and novels? This answer not only reveals a lot about your vision, it also reveals what feeds and forms it. We tend to become what we consume. If your focus is the sports page, over time you will value people with athletic ability. If you enjoy reading about the latest actresses and fashions, appearance will become increasingly important to you. If you find yourself consuming the latest hunting magazines, hunting will grow in your heart and control more of your vision. It is important to determine what is feeding and forming your vision. Is it being formed by the world or the Word?

Life is amazingly short. When you are young, time passes slowly and life seems endless. It is normal to find enjoyment in activities like volleyball or softball for a while, but as you mature, God is calling you to a vision much higher than just living for personal pleasure. You are on a path and moving toward a destiny. Your vision largely determines what you accomplish in life and where you end up. God wants to transform that vision. He is trying to take your gaze off yourself and focus it on His Kingdom. In short, He wants you to have a Kingdom vision.

A Kingdom Vision

But what is a Kingdom vision? Perhaps the best way to illustrate is by starting with an infant. Babies are transparent. They have not learned to hide their feelings. When they get hungry, they let you know. When they have a need, they make it known. They haven't learned subtlety. They just let you know how they feel, usually quite vocally.

What drives an infant? What is his motivating force? It is self, isn't it? Have you ever seen a three-month-old child cry because another child was hungry? Have you ever seen him worry because of a need in someone else's life? No, infants don't do that. Their only concern is how every event affects them. We could say they live for the "kingdom of self." Every incident throughout the day is judged by how it affects their "kingdom." If self is hungry, food is good. If self doesn't want food right now, food isn't good. An infant's life is consumed with the kingdom of self.

God desires that we have that same passion for the Kingdom of God. A man with a Kingdom vision views every event according to how it affects the Kingdom of God. Isn't this what inspires us about those early disciples? As we read those first chapters in the book of Acts, isn't the change of focus and vision what captivates us? Just before the crucifixion they were running for their lives. They were so intent on saving their skins, they forsook Jesus and hid. Peter repeatedly lied, and another disciple even left his clothes behind as he made a desperate dash for freedom. Life was about self.

But after the resurrection something changed. The disciples caught a glimpse of something powerful—something more valuable and glorious than living for self. They caught a vision of the Kingdom of God, and their lives were never the same again. No longer did they judge each daily event by how it affected them. They viewed their own feelings, fears, and wants as unimportant. As Paul later told the church at Philippi, "But what things were gain to me, those I counted loss for Christ."[a] Paul went on to say that all the things he once viewed as valuable he now regarded as worthless as a pile of manure.

Paul received a vision of living for the Kingdom of God. All the things that at one time had captivated and enthralled him now appeared cheap and worthless. This same Kingdom vision can motivate and transform your life.

Conclusion

Sonya Carson's life demonstrates what a motivating vision can do. Surrounded by crime, poverty, and discouragement, she was able to visualize possibilities. But she did not just sit and think. Sonya got up and put her dreams into action. Night after night she encouraged and worked with her boys, helping them rise out of the Detroit slums.

In many ways your situation resembles Sonya's. You also live in a discouraging world. Your society, like hers, is spiraling downward. You will be surrounded daily by disheartening situations. But like Sonya Carson, you can picture something better. The very best this world has to offer ends at death. All the entertainment, fashion, and possessions people chase will be worthless the day after their funeral.

"THE VERY BEST THIS WORLD HAS TO OFFER ENDS AT DEATH. ALL THE ENTERTAINMENT, FASHION, AND POSSESSIONS PEOPLE CHASE WILL BE WORTHLESS THE DAY AFTER THEIR FUNERAL."

But God is calling you to a higher vision, much higher than climbing out of the Detroit slums. God is calling you to embrace the Kingdom vision of those early disciples. He is asking your generation to

[a]Philippians 3:7

renounce the love of this world and show by your daily choices that this world is not your home. He is calling you, in your youth, to focus all your resources on living for Him and building His Kingdom. Let that vision penetrate your heart. Let it be the motivating force in your life, and be willing to renounce anything that competes.

For Further Reflection

1. What would you do if you suddenly received $1,000?
2. What would you do if you were given a week to do what you want?
3. What do your answers to these questions reveal about your vision?
4. What are some ways we can demonstrate a different vision to the materialistic culture around us?

"Choose You This Day" | 3

. . . BUT AS FOR ME AND MY HOUSE, WE WILL SERVE THE LORD.
JOSHUA 24:15

It must have been a weary Joshua who stood before the people that day. They had seen God's power manifested in miraculous ways, witnessed the walls of Jericho falling, and watched God drive powerful enemies out of the land before them. But still they doubted. Still they looked back and were tempted to lean on false gods from their past. Joshua stood before them once again as his life was coming to a close and pleaded with them.

"Choose you this day,"[a] he told them. "Make a final decision for yourselves and your families. Quit trying to serve the Lord with one hand and idols with the other. Make a choice!"

As Joshua spoke to the people that day, his mind must have gone back to the last days of Moses' life. It must have seemed like yesterday that an exasperated Moses had stood before these people and pleaded with them. He too had asked them to make a choice.

"See, I have set before thee this day life and good, and death and evil," Moses had said. "I call heaven and earth to record this day against you, that I have set before you life and death, blessing and cursing: therefore choose life, that both thou and thy seed mayest live."[b]

Now Joshua was standing where Moses had stood. This was getting redundant! Here he was at the end of his life telling the people once again, "Choose you this day whom you will serve!"

God's Continual Cry

All through the Bible God has pleaded with man to make a choice.

[a]Joshua 24:15
[b]Deuteronomy 30:15, 19

Elijah stood on Mount Carmel and asked the people a similar question: "How long halt ye between two opinions?"[c] In other words, "When are you going to decide once and for all?" Years later Jeremiah laid this same issue out before the people of his day: "Behold, I set before you the way of life, and the way of death."[d]

All through history God has asked His people to make a clean break with the gods of this world and give allegiance to Him alone. And all through history we have tried to serve both. While this temptation follows us all our lives, Satan seems to work hardest with the young. If he can convince you to begin walking down the well-worn path of compromise in your youth, he knows his task will be much easier.

The Creative Compromiser

The story is told of a man who built his house across the Arkansas-Missouri state line. For years the county officials in Arkansas thought he was paying his taxes in Missouri, and the Missouri officials assumed he was paying his taxes in Arkansas. This went on for some time until finally it was discovered he was not paying taxes in either!

Officials from both states got together and investigated the regulations, and a law was uncovered that addressed this dilemma. It said a man must pay taxes in the state he actually sleeps in. So one night officers from both states, after some cooperative discussion,

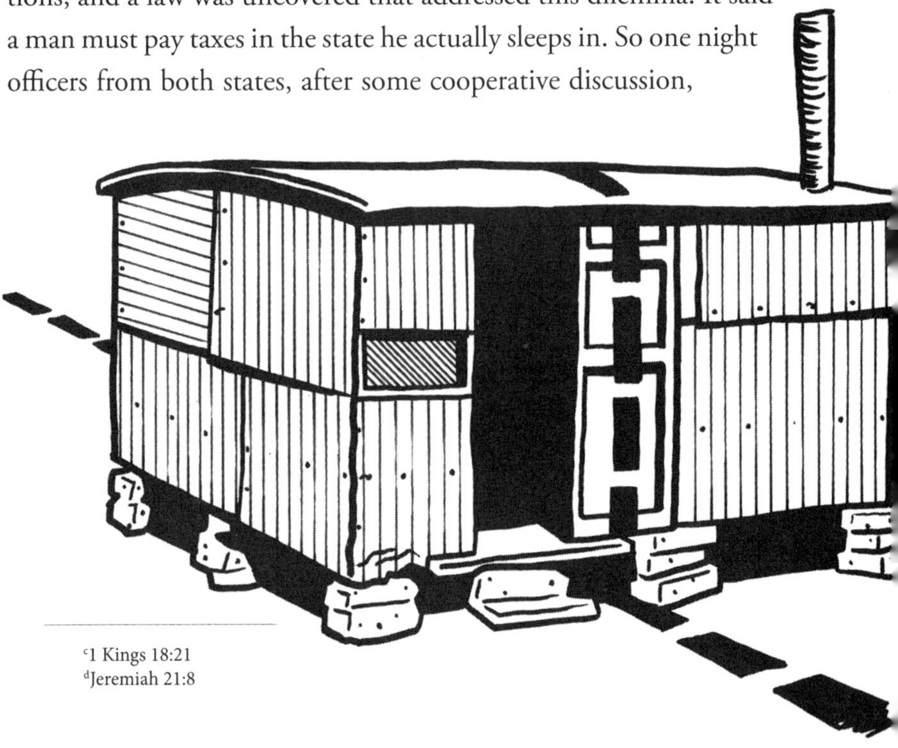

[c]1 Kings 18:21
[d]Jeremiah 21:8

crept up to the house to discover where this man slept. To their amazement, the crafty old codger had placed his bed directly across the state line as well!

Sometimes as young believers we are like the devious tax dodger. Parts of our lives profess loyalty to one kingdom and parts to another. We like to speak of walking in the light while actually living in the shadows.

To Whom Do You Belong?

Before we look at the details of our finances and how money is to be used, it is important to do some self-examination. To whom do you really belong? As professing believers in the Lord Jesus, we have all openly stated our allegiance to Jesus Christ. We have said we are willing to surrender everything for Him. But are you really? As we approach the area of finances, are you willing to let the Word of God dictate how your money is used? Are you willing to allow the Spirit of God to lead you in this area?

> DOES GOD REALLY CARE HOW I SPEND THAT TWENTY-DOLLAR BILL IN MY WALLET?

Many of us have grown up in Christian homes. We have watched how our parents used their money. We have observed how they regard possessions. But have you ever wondered how God views the issue? Does He have an opinion on possessions? Does God really care how I spend that twenty-dollar bill in my wallet?

Maybe you feel you have a good grasp on money and finances. But is it possible you have been deceived by our culture? We have been raised in one of the most prosperous times in history and grown up in the midst of great affluence. Are you sure you are looking at wealth, possessions, and ownership correctly? Are you looking at money as Jesus does? Dealing with money every day creates challenges for all of us. We have to use it, yet Jesus clearly tells us it is dangerous. It would be good to go back and look at some of Jesus' basic teachings. After all, if we have declared our allegiance to Him, we will surely want to examine closely what He taught.

Jesus said much about money and riches. He almost seems preoccupied with the topic. He used riches in His parables to illustrate truths. He talked about those who were wealthy as well as those who were poor. He taught about borrowing money and instructed those who lent. He talked about giving—about giving in secret and sharing even if one had little to give. Jesus even said that our Father puts treasure into an account in heaven when we share with the poor here on earth. He talked about the emptiness of stockpiling wealth in this world and the consequences of idleness and slothfulness.

In fact, it has been said that Jesus talked more about wealth than almost any other topic. Why is this? Why so much focus on money and possessions? Why did Jesus say we could not serve God and mammon? Is it possible that Jesus saw dangers in riches that we have ignored?

I believe He did.

But before we look at the danger Jesus saw, let's consider the desires of young people today. Let's look at your longings. What is it you crave in those quiet moments of meditation when it seems no one understands? You may think you are alone and no one else feels as you do. But consider the following areas and see you if you can identify with these basic desires.

- Acceptance. Do you ever wonder if others in your peer group really appreciate you? Are there times when you just wish your friends would accept you for who you are? Every young man and woman wants acceptance. We like to walk up to a group of young people and feel like we belong. There is nothing like that warm feeling of acceptance. There is also nothing quite as miserable as feeling we don't belong and are not accepted. It's universal—we long for acceptance.

- Security. With all the uncertainty and constant change that surrounds you, do you ever long for stability? Do you ever wish life would stop changing? We all like to know we are secure. We like to feel secure in our families, at school, and in our churches. Every small child loves the feeling of security that comes from snuggling in his mother's arms. Sometimes as we get older and life gets more uncertain, we long for that sense of security we felt as children.

- Happiness. We might have trouble defining happiness, but we all know when we are happy. It is a mixture of pleasure, gladness, and contentment that cannot be hidden. The man who is happy bubbles over with it. Sometimes it seems elusive, but we all desire happiness.

- Power. While men may have a stronger craving for power than women do, I think at times we all want power, regardless of gender. Whether we are trying to hit a ball or have our way in a relationship, we like what power does for us. There is a certain thrill that comes with it, something about being able to prevail and conquer.

This list could go on and on. We could look at feelings like love, fulfillment, and influence. As humans, we understand and long for all of these. We all have the same basic desires.

The God of Mammon

The god of mammon or money offers to fulfill every one of these desires. He promises all this and more if we will only serve him. He tempts us with images and with words. *Just look what I have done for the wealthy men and women of the world. Because they have worked hard and faithfully served me, I have given them wealth and possessions, acceptance, security, happiness, and power. They are people of power and influence simply because they have served me!*

We are surrounded by this message daily, and as a young man or woman you will need to respond in some way to this god of mammon. He is a powerful god. He has many gifts to offer. The god of mammon promises to protect and provide security as long as this life lasts. If you pick up most books in the self-help section of the bookstore, you will find more of this god's claims.

I remember thinking as a young man, "If a man just has enough money, nothing can overcome him." I couldn't think of many problems life could throw at me that money could not take care of. This is the offer of the god of mammon (who, as many have discovered, does not always deliver what he promises).

The Call of Jesus

But the god of mammon is not the only god offering these gifts. Jesus has offered to fulfill these same desires in those who are willing to follow Him. If you are struggling with acceptance or insecurity, Jesus can fill that need. Notice His offer: "If a man love me, he will keep my words: and my Father will love him, and we will come unto him, and make our abode with him."[e] This is an amazing promise. What could be more powerful than having the God of the universe living with you? Jesus has promised to take care of every need if you follow Him. If you want to have spiritual power or leave a godly influence, Jesus has promised that through Him we can do anything.

There is an ongoing battle between the god of mammon and the God of the universe. Both have made their proposals. The one offers immediate pleasure but gives no hope after this life. The other asks for sacrifice today but promises unspeakable joy tomorrow. One requires only feelings; the other takes faith.

But there is another difference between these two proposals, and this is the burden of this chapter. Let me illustrate it like this. When I was first attracted to my wife, we began to spend more time together, usually in a group setting with other young people. We were just friends. Even though we never talked about it, we understood; I was simply one of her many friends.

But the time finally came that I asked her to be my wife. We both understood this was different. There was an understanding that she was to be my only wife and I was to be her only husband. We have

[e]John 14:23

many friends, but only one spouse.

The call of Jesus is the same. He demands total allegiance and love. While the god of mammon may not care if you pursue other gods, Jesus does. He is very clear. We cannot serve God and mammon.

Conclusion

God is calling you to make a choice. Will you serve Almighty God and devote your life to Him regardless of the cost? Or will you serve this present world, money, and possessions? Too often we are like the crafty old tax evader. We try to place our bed on the state line. When we are with the popular group, we want to appear popular, and when we are with the spiritual group we want to look spiritual. Sometimes in our teenage years it is possible to find a "compromising group," where we can become comfortable living a double life.

But make no mistake. God is not mocked, and He hates hypocrisy and compromise. Let the world, your fellow workers, and everyone you come in contact with know where you belong and whom you serve. Let every part of your life—from your appearance to your work ethic to your use of money—declare plainly that your life has been bought with a price. Make it clear that you belong to Jesus Christ and have renounced the god of mammon, "for ye serve the Lord Christ!"[f]

For Further Reflection

1. Share some examples of ways we can be hypocritical—times when our words and actions give conflicting messages.

2. List some differences between Jesus' teachings on wealth and possessions and the messages we get from our society on the subject.

3. Share examples of ways you have tried to gain acceptance or happiness by acquiring something.

4. List some problems in life that money cannot alleviate.

[f]Colossians 3:24

Biblical Stewardship— The Missing Ingredient? 4

A CHECKBOOK IS A THEOLOGICAL DOCUMENT;
IT WILL TELL YOU WHO AND WHAT YOU WORSHIP.
—BILLY GRAHAM

Sally grew up with unbelieving parents. Her life was a cycle of school activities, trips to the mall, and television. She lived in a quiet Midwestern suburb, her father was successful, and she was popular among her peers. Many looking on would have seen just another American girl, but something was going on inside that others could not see.

As I listened to Sally's[a] story several years ago, I was impressed by this young woman's desire for and pursuit of truth. In the community where she grew up there was a fellowship of Bible-believing followers of the Lord Jesus. Sally was curious as she watched these people. She observed how they interacted and cared for each other. She noticed the women's cheerful countenances in the supermarkets and the strange white veils on their heads. And she heard the stories.

People around town said these folks were different. Really different! It was rumored they did not even have televisions in their homes. Amazing! Sally wondered what life would be like without television. But that was not all. They didn't even attend things like fairs or parades, and they stayed away from normal activities like movies and professional sporting events. But Sally saw something else in these people. They had an inner tranquility and an outer glow that she desired. As Sally listened to the stories and watched how they lived, she wondered: *Who are these strange people? Why have they chosen to live so differently?*

A few years went by and Sally finally had an opportunity to inquire.

[a]Names and details of stories have been changed throughout the book to protect identity.

She began working with a young girl who wore one of those strange veils on her head, and Sally began to ask questions—lots of questions. "Why do you wear that thing on your head? Why don't you go to movies? Do you get bored in the evening without television? Why don't you wear jewelry?" Day after day her new friend cheerfully tried to answer all these questions.

This Stuff Is in the Bible!

As Sally pondered all she was being told, she began to notice something. Almost every time she asked a question, her friend referred to some part of the Bible. Of course, Sally had a Bible in her home. Didn't every good American have one? As Sally's friend gave references in answer to her questions, Sally began to look them up, and she was amazed. There really was basic, understandable teaching in the Bible!

All of this led Sally to spend time in the Word of God, and as she read, the Spirit worked. After several years she reached a point of decision, and she chose to commit her life to the Lord Jesus. She chose to follow even though it changed almost every part of her daily life. Sally walked away from the old life she had grown up in and embraced this new life in Christ. Reluctant at first, her family eventually accepted her decision, and Sally found inner joy and peace and became a radiant example for Jesus in her community.

Several years had passed since her conversion when I met Sally, and now she had more questions. She had initially been attracted to Christianity by the people in her neighborhood who lived very different lives. They possessed something within that she wanted. So Sally had counted the cost. She had looked at what she might lose in friendships, appearance, and standing in her community. And she had chosen to give it all up for her Lord Jesus. Her church leaders had encouraged her to keep reading her Bible. "Keep searching God's Word," they had told her, "and the Holy Spirit will give you further direction." So Sally did.

The Questions

Occasionally Sally would read a passage in the Bible she did not understand. Whenever this happened, she would meet with her church leaders and ask about it. She appreciated their openness. When she asked them about turning the other cheek, she was impressed with their answer. They said it meant exactly what it said. Even if we are persecuted or imprisoned, we must not fight back. They told stories of many martyrs who had died rather than abandon this teaching.

When Sally asked about divorce and remarriage, using the courts to defend ourselves, or taking oaths, their answer was always the same. "We just do what the Bible says," the church leaders told her. "The Bible is not that complicated. Even a child can understand what these verses mean." This was the kind of fellowship she wanted to be part of. Just read the Bible and do what it says.

But then she began asking about money.

This One Is Different

Abruptly the answers began to sound a little different. Suddenly things were not quite as clear, and Sally became confused. She read all that Jesus said about money and wealth. She examined His teachings and warnings about laying up treasures. She studied what He taught about how money should be regarded, about lending not hoping to receive it again, and about giving to every man who asked. Then she began to look at the lifestyles within her fellowship.

Sally's unbelieving father had been a saver. He loved to plan, invest, and map out the future. He could tell you how setting aside a little money each month for retirement could add up to a fortune over time. When he retired, he planned to have plenty of money to travel and do the things he had always longed to do.

Now as Sally listened to the older men and women in her congregation, it sounded like an echo of her unbelieving father. The older members in her congregation were also looking forward to the day they wouldn't have to go to work anymore. Just like her dad, they were saving, investing, and trying to amass wealth. Many times she overheard them discussing the safest places to put money, the best way to buy a farm, and the best places in Florida to retire. In spite of all Jesus had said about laying up wealth, they talked just like her dad!

No wonder Sally was confused! On most topics her leaders taught that a follower of Jesus should do just what Jesus said. They taught her that even though the cost of radical discipleship can be great, we are to trust God and obey. This made their lives very different from the surrounding culture. It made them act, look, and respond differently. But in the area of wealth and possessions, it seemed the businessmen in her congregation operated very much like the world around them. True, they were known for their honesty and good work ethic, and when people in the community wanted to hire someone, they knew who could be trusted. But her fellow church members chased that dollar just as hard as anyone else. Jesus had warned against riches and the accumulation of goods, yet those in her congregation who had accumulated the most were also the most highly regarded. Some of her fellow church members had accumulated more wealth than the average unbeliever. Their farms were larger and their businesses more successful. In fact, her church was known for being wealthy!

"WHY DO WE CONSIDER THE TEACHINGS OF JESUS REGARDING MONEY DIFFERENT THAN OTHER DIFFICULT TEACHINGS HE GAVE?"

So Sally asked, "Why is wealth different? Why do we consider the teachings of Jesus regarding money different than other difficult teachings He gave? Why do we focus so strongly on some issues and then make excuses for this one? Why?"

We Have Failed

Maybe you have a good answer for Sally's question. But I think most of us who are living in America agree we have failed. As I look at my own struggle in dealing with wealth and materialism, I freely admit to hypocrisy. I have talked about the inconsistency in others, and yet the Lord has faithfully revealed, and continues to expose, my own. I have regarded with scorn the high level of living among professing Christians, and then come face to face with my own self-centeredness and hypocrisy. I have acted more like an owner than a steward. I have thought of possessions and money as mine, not God's.

As you begin your Christian life and consider making your own choices, how do you view the things you "own"? How do you regard "your" money in the bank? Do you think of money as something that belongs to you and is for your good? Or are you simply a steward, constantly listening for instructions from the real Owner? These questions are not easy. They cannot always be answered quickly. We need to take them before the Lord, and I firmly believe the best time to do so is while you are young.

Something Missing?

Most people have a cooking story about something that did not turn out right. Maybe too much or too little of an ingredient was used, or perhaps one was forgotten altogether. But whatever it is, the end product does not come out right. Everyone sits around the dinner table and no one wants to state the obvious. Something is missing! Oh, yes, it looks good and smells right, but something just isn't as it should be.

Is it possible that an improper view of Biblical stewardship is part of our problem with evangelism? Could it be the missing ingredient in our witness to the world? We say all the right things. We have ready answers for the skeptics' questions, and we can explain why our church is better than other churches. But the fact is, when considering wealth and possessions, our lives bear little resemblance to the Man we say we are following. He didn't even have a bed of His own; we are known for our large homes. He taught against accumulating wealth; we are known for large farms and big businesses. His teaching on wealth was radically different from His culture; ours sounds amazingly similar to our culture. How many more confused Sallys are out there?

How many people like the message we bring them, but lose interest when they observe our lives? How many even show some initial curiosity, but are eventually turned off when they find our lives are not that different after all when it comes to how we regard money? These are sobering questions. Perhaps we need to go back and reexamine the teachings of the Man we say we are imitating.

Conclusion

While this chapter has focused primarily on failure in the older generation, we also have some shining examples in our congregations of people who have made deliberate choices to live for the Kingdom. I think of Carl and Edna, a couple whose lives have been a demonstration of reaching out in compassion. With eight children of their own already, they adopted four others from a single-parent home and poured their time and energy into pointing them toward the Kingdom.

> PERHAPS WE NEED TO GO BACK AND REEXAMINE THE TEACHINGS OF THE MAN WE SAY WE ARE IMITATING.

Then there's David and Miriam, who late in life received a large sum of money from the sale of their successful business. After laboring year after year, they now had the resources to pursue any hobby they desired, buy any kind of vehicle they wanted, or spend time vacationing in exotic locations around the globe. They could do whatever they wanted!

And what did they do? They still drove the same older vehicle and channeled all of that money into helping widows and orphans and into producing literature to reach people who had never heard the Gospel.

These people have made deliberate choices to live for the Kingdom, and now their example inspires others.

You also have the opportunity in your youth to establish a Biblical vision for your life and finances. By beginning while you are young, you can focus on Kingdom building your entire lifetime.

Young people growing up in conservative churches tend to have more money at their disposal than the average youth in society (though it should be noted that in many homes part of a young person's income goes to help support his or her family). Most are taught good work ethics in their youth. This usually makes it easy to find work in our increasingly lazy society. In addition, most fellowships have a network of businesses, and rarely is anyone unemployed for long. When a young man needs work, he can usually pick up the phone and call others in his community and soon have all the work he needs.

All of this translates into young people with more available cash than many their age in the community. This can be a blessing to the Kingdom if it is channeled there, but it can also become a snare.

For Further Reflection

1. How does the average member in your congregation compare financially with the rest of your community? Is there a difference?

2. How do you compare financially with non-Christian youth in your community?

3. Have we neglected focusing on the teachings of Jesus on stewardship and wealth? If so, share some possible reasons this has occurred.

4. How would it impact your community if unbelievers knew that wealth and possessions held little attraction for you?

Do I View Money and Possessions as Jesus Does? | 5

WHY CALL YE ME, LORD, LORD, AND
DO NOT THE THINGS WHICH I SAY?
LUKE 6:46

A couple of years ago I visited a very poor area in the Dominican Republic, where I saw a few boys playing baseball on the street. All they had was a crooked branch for a bat and a green lime for a ball. But they had a rousing game going in spite of that, and they knew the rules. I was intrigued by how universal baseball rules are. Here they were, surrounded by poverty and desperate need, yet they knew that each batter got only three strikes with that crooked stick.

Not every game is the same. Each game has its own set of rules. We understand, for example, that you are not allowed to grab the basketball and run to the other end of the court. The ball must be dribbled as you run. But in football just the opposite is true. If you can get your hands on the ball, it is imperative that you run as fast as possible toward the end zone without letting the ball touch the ground. We don't try to apply one set of rules to a different game. We might not know who came up with the rules, why some of them exist, or who to talk to if we want to change them, but if we want to play the game, we accept the rules. No matter how famous a baseball player is or how much money he brings home a year, he is still required to tag all the bases while running for home plate. Regardless of who you are, you play by the rules.

Though we understand this truth in sports, we have difficulty applying the concept to the Word of God. We accept without question that the volleyball must go over the net, yet wonder if we are really required to follow all of God's commands. The Bible is clear on many issues. There is no shortage of instruction, for example, on divorce and remarriage. Yet "Christianity" has had a tendency to gradually modify the rules on many of these Biblical doctrines.

Life will be over someday, and at the final judgment we will stand before God, not the religious authorities of our day. With this in view, develop a passion for truth while you are young. Search it out for yourself and ask God to direct your steps. Study the many teachings Jesus gave regarding wealth and possessions. When we accept Jesus, we accept His teachings.

WHEN WE ACCEPT JESUS, WE ACCEPT HIS TEACHINGS.

I Want Truth Now!

God is sovereign and His decisions are final, so it is extremely important for us to find out what God thinks. As we approach this topic of money, these should be our first questions: What does God think? What has He said? What are the rules? How does He regard our use of possessions and money?

We all like to think we have a proper understanding of life. We see others who tend to be imbalanced, but we like to believe we have a balanced view. But too often we create our points of reference from those around us rather than listening to God Himself. Since childhood we have observed how our parents regard their money. We watch what kinds of things our friends buy and what is important to them. We hear good teaching at church services regarding giving and the foolishness of storing up wealth. But we also see how people around us actually live, and slowly their values become our values. We hear people say, "That man is successful." They mean he makes a lot of money. So we learn to equate money with success.

As we consider our values and the importance of using money and possessions correctly, we need to ask ourselves: "Do I view financial issues as Jesus does?" Jesus Himself will judge us on that final day, so it is of utmost importance that we investigate what Jesus taught on this topic.

Jesus' Teachings

There is no shortage of information regarding what Jesus believed about money. He worked money into much of His teaching and many of His illustrations. But sometimes we can learn the most by watching how Jesus responded to situations and comparing His response to what we would do. We learn how to love by seeing how He responded as the nails were driven through His hands. We learn how to live under our parents' authority by watching Jesus return home from Jerusalem as a twelve-year-old. The Bible says He returned "and was subject unto them."[a] In the same way, we can learn something from His response to money.

Let's look first at the account regarding the man we refer to as the rich young ruler.[b] This man came to Jesus with a serious concern. He wanted to make sure he was going to inherit eternal life. He had an important question, and he came to the right source for answers. Since the time he was just a little boy, he had honored his parents. How many other men his age could say that? He had not been involved in immorality, theft, or lying. And not only that, this man was serious about his spirituality. He was not focusing only on the natural; he was looking ahead to the time after death. He wanted to be certain about his future. He was also an eager learner. The Bible does not say this man was just standing there in the crowd one day when he thought of a question. No, he came specifically to ask this question. Mark even says the man came running. He really wanted to learn!

How Does Jesus' View Compare With Mine?

Now remember, we want to see if your view of money and possessions is the same as Jesus'. Imagine for a moment you are the minister of a church. You are sitting at home one evening, and a young man stops in with a question. He has a few doubts and wants to be sure he is saved and going to heaven when he dies. You know this young man. You have watched him grow up in your congregation. You have observed his respectful attitude toward his parents. This young man has always lived an upright life, and you can still remember the day

[a]Luke 2:51
[b]Luke 18:18-27

when he gave his life to the Lord Jesus. He has a sincere desire to know more about the Lord. If there's a prayer meeting or Bible study, he is the first one there.

This young man has also been very diligent in business and has obvious leadership skills. It seems that everything he touches turns a profit. If there is any concern at all, it is that he seems so interested in getting ahead financially. Now he is sitting in your living room and has a serious question. "Am I really saved? If I die, will I go to heaven?"

How would you answer this question? Think for a moment about all the possible responses you might give him. You have seen his weakness in the area of business, but can you really imagine telling him to sell everything he has? Can you imagine telling anyone that?

Are We Serious About Covetousness?

We know how to respond when a church member falls into open and unrepentant immorality. We believe the church should act quickly and decisively. If a member is caught stealing, we feel strongly that the church should respond. But somehow when a man's passion is his business, we don't know quite what to do. When an individual is focused on obtaining more farmland or going deeper into debt to expand his business, we are not sure how to approach the situation. And what about the young man who continually adds unneeded accessories to his vehicle? Or the young woman who keeps buying shoes and clothing, though she already has trouble shutting her closet door? The point here is not to find fault. The question is, do we view money and possessions as Jesus did? We have much less fear of wealth than Jesus' warnings might call for. Covetousness and desire for wealth are listed in the New Testament right along with fornication, theft, and murder. Yet I find myself, in our capitalistic culture, not fearing wealth as I do immorality. We need to examine our values by the Word of God. It is important to get our understanding on these issues from the Bible and not from society.

Just Two Mites

Let's look at another account. Jesus was sitting in the temple one day watching the people donate money.[c] The Bible says that rich men were casting their gifts into the temple treasury. We can see them lined up, carrying their bags of coins and pouring money into the treasury. Imagine for a moment you are the chief treasurer for the temple. It is your job to make sure there is enough money in the account and that all the bills are paid each month. It takes a lot of money to operate the temple, and you rejoice to see the big givers arrive. Your eyes scan the line for the big bags, and when the large donations pour into the coffers, the clinking of coins sounds like music to your ears.

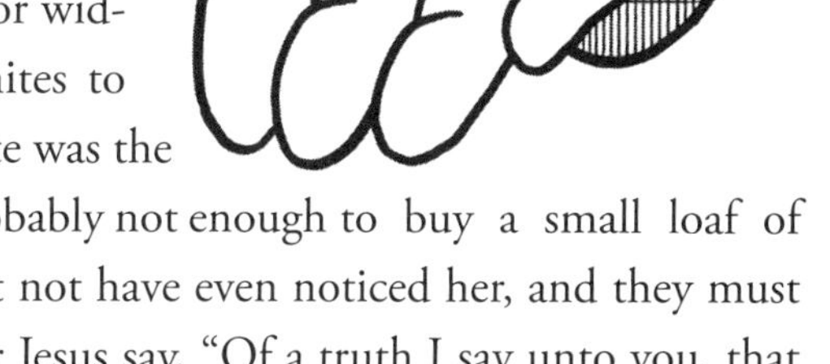

But while Jesus watched this parade of wealthy men pass the offering box, He pointed out a poor widow who had only two mites to give. Just two mites! A mite was the smallest coin they had, probably not enough to buy a small loaf of bread. The disciples might not have even noticed her, and they must have been shocked to hear Jesus say, "Of a truth I say unto you, that this poor widow hath cast in more than they all."[d]

Does that make sense to you? We have grown up hearing this story. We have heard many lessons about the widow and the two mites and how the Lord loves sacrificial giving. But just for a moment, back away from this story and let's think about the message and values taught here. Let's consider our own setting today.

What Do I Really Value?

With this account of the widow and her two mites still in our minds, let's consider a few questions. I want you to analyze your value system,

[c]Luke 21:1
[d]Luke 21:3

and to do this we will compare two people. One is this poor widow. She had only two mites, and she gave them to the Lord. The other person we want to consider is Bill Gates. Mr. Gates started Microsoft and has been one of the wealthiest men in the world for years. These two represent the two ends of the spectrum. One represents heavenly wealth, the other earthly.

If you had an opportunity to interview or spend a day with someone, would you rather meet Bill Gates or this poor widow? Which person would intrigue and interest you? Which one would you consider successful? Which one would you say is a wise investor? One has billions of dollars at his disposal on earth, and the other has sent everything on to heaven. Which one do you honestly regard as a wise investor?

I think most of us would have to agree that we have been impacted heavily by our culture. I have read all these Biblical accounts from my youth, yet I still find myself intrigued by those with earthly wealth. I am attracted to newspaper articles that describe the lifestyles of the rich. This tells me that earthly wealth still holds a certain attraction and place in my heart. The bottom line is, I do not yet regard wealth and possessions as Jesus does. I do not have a proper fear of riches and the effect they can have on my heart.

Conclusion

All of us have reference points in our lives. We use these to interpret life and make decisions. It is important to begin using correct reference points while you are young. Our culture tells us that money and possessions are important—that the person who has the most of these things has the greatest value. Jesus said just the opposite. He taught that the man who is really wise will give to the poor and have treasure in heaven. You need to decide which reference point to use—the words of Jesus or the surrounding culture.

God's Word does not move. He is the One who sets the rules. You can choose to ignore this. You can rest in the fact that many people are ignoring God and pursuing wealth. But when the whistle blows, God's rules will prevail. God's Word is very clear on this topic. The Apostle Paul said those who have a desire to be rich will ultimately drown in destruction and perdition.[e] Visualize how silly it would be for a batter to argue with the umpire after swinging and missing the ball three times. "I know I swung three times," he argues, "but I've always thought it should be four strikes before you're out." The batter would be laughed off the field. How much more foolish it is to argue with the almighty God of the universe!

For Further Reflection

1. List some areas where modern Christianity has ignored basic Scriptural teaching. What are some examples in which we have done the same?

2. What comments do we make that convey to the listener that we regard money and possessions highly?

3. How have Jesus' teachings impacted your financial life? Can you think of times you have chosen a different path because of one of His teachings?

4. Jesus gave some strong warnings against wealth. If a man had a healthy fear of wealth, describe what his life might look like. What steps might he take to avoid becoming ensnared?

5. Discuss the importance of developing good reference points in our lives in the area of wealth and possessions. How can we do this? What are some steps we can take in our youth to help us begin to view wealth as Jesus did?

[e] 1 Timothy 6:9

Developing a Biblical Value System 6

BUT LAY UP FOR YOURSELVES TREASURES IN HEAVEN,
WHERE NEITHER MOTH NOR RUST DOTH CORRUPT.
MATTHEW 6:20

Just a few miles from our home is a large junkyard. It's out close to the road, and as I drive into town I cannot help but ponder the sight. Junkyards tend to be eyesores. People don't like to look at them, so usually the local government requires a privacy fence to help the appearance of the neighborhood. Something about the chaos and disorder, piles of smashed cars, and weeds growing up through old vehicles repels us. But I wonder sometimes if we wouldn't be further ahead in our Christian life if we spent more time in junkyards.

Perhaps you have never considered having your morning devotions in a junkyard, but I'd like for you to try it. Junkyards have some tremendous lessons to teach us. Driving by our local junkyard, I can see a Pontiac Grand Am resting on top of another vehicle too damaged to recognize. A white Dodge Neon with a smashed hood sticks up in the air, its rear doors missing, its rear tires astride the remains of a luxury vehicle. Chevy and Ford trucks, probably owned by young men who argued over which was the best, now lie side by side, rusting together. Volkswagens and limousines, taxis and old airport shuttles—everything shares a certain sameness.

"CHEVY AND FORD TRUCKS, PROBABLY OWNED BY YOUNG MEN WHO ARGUED OVER WHICH WAS THE BEST, NOW LIE SIDE BY SIDE, RUSTING TOGETHER."

Junkyard Meditations

Recently I pulled off the side of the road and spent some time thinking about the lessons in the junkyard. I looked at the remains of a black Nissan Maxima. It had come with every option available—aluminum wheels, a sunroof, leather seats . . . I tried to imagine the day, not too many years ago, when someone had driven it off the lot. I pictured him driving home, excited and impatient to show his friends. I imagined the effort he might have put into protecting it from scratches and dents. I visualized the Saturdays spent polishing those aluminum wheels, waxing that beautiful shiny paint, cleaning the leather interior, and buffing those chrome accent strips. Now the windows are open and rain comes in through the open sunroof. This car, which just a few years ago probably wouldn't have been left outside overnight, is now completely unprotected from the elements and is deteriorating rapidly. I wondered if its original owner ever thinks about it. Here is a possession that at one time was very valuable to him. He was willing to make great sacrifices to obtain it, but now it has almost no value. It is junk.

Lessons From the Junkyard

What can we learn from the junkyard? Many good meditations can come from these piles of rusting metal, but I would like to focus on two simple lessons:

- Every earthly possession ends up being junk. Take a little time to look around you. Think about the great value men and women place on things. Regardless of how things are regarded by society, everything you can see is ultimately going to deteriorate. Nothing is exempt. Bodies end up in graveyards, and things wind up in junkyards or landfills. Remember this as you consider what to buy and where to invest your money.

- True value is determined only by usefulness. In a junkyard it is easy to conclude that things have no value and just don't matter. But those airport shuttles were valuable at one time to those who needed to get to the airport. Our problem with possessions is that we assign more value to items than their usefulness calls for. Too often we assign value to items simply because we perceive that others think they are valuable. But in the end the junkyard gets it right. Scrap metal from a limousine sells for the same price per pound as scrap metal from an old clunker.

> BUT IN THE END THE JUNKYARD GETS IT RIGHT. SCRAP METAL FROM A LIMOUSINE SELLS FOR THE SAME PRICE PER POUND AS SCRAP METAL FROM AN OLD CLUNKER.

Analyze your values. Don't put your affection on things bound for the junkyard. Take a quick inventory of your life. What are you willing to invest your time, money, and effort into? Are any of these items junkyard bound? Are you loving and pursuing anything that will one day rust? What is the final destination of the things you value? At times you need items that will ultimately end up in the junkyard. You can't help that. But make every effort not to set your heart on things that will deteriorate.

What Did Jesus Say?

It is imperative that you start with the Bible to develop a Biblical value system. Too often we live as though the Bible is silent on the topic of finances, but let's look at some of its teachings on this topic. Jesus gave so many warnings against wealth that we could easily conclude that we should stay away from money—that we should regard money as evil and avoid it as much as possible.

Men have tried this. Throughout history there have been men who walked away from society and tried to avoid people and commerce, isolating themselves so they would not have to bother with the everyday struggles that plague humanity. We call them hermits. But is this really what God has in mind? Does He intend that we totally avoid commerce and money?

No. It is evident from Paul's teaching that God intends for us to both earn money and invest it. Notice Paul's words to the church at Ephesus: "Let him that stole steal no more: but rather let him labour, working with his hands the thing which is good, that he may have to give to him that needeth."[a]

Four distinct teachings in this little verse provide an important window into the heart of God regarding labor, money, and His ultimate purpose for our endeavors in the world of commerce.

First, we are to seek money ethically. Paul says we are not to steal or seek gain unjustly. Second, we are to earn by laboring diligently with our hands. Many other Scriptures address this truth as well. Paul reiterated this to the church at Thessalonica when he said "that if any would not work, neither should he eat."[b] God desires for us to be diligent and industrious. He intends that we have an occupation. A slothful, lazy attitude has no place among God's children.

But not just any occupation will do. Notice Paul's next point. He says that we should be engaged in a "thing which is good." Many occupations bring in a large income. But are they a blessing to our communities? Is it a "thing which is good"? We need to be engaged in commerce that blesses our neighbors and is a good witness to our community.

---

[a]Ephesians 4:28
[b]2 Thessalonians 3:10

Finally, Paul says the purpose of this is to give to him that needeth. This means that God desires that we accomplish more than just providing for our own households. He intends that we bless others, specifically the poor. Jesus described this kind of alms giving as a good investment. Notice His words as you consider sharing with the poor: "Sell that ye have, and give alms; provide yourselves bags which wax not old, a treasure in the heavens that faileth not, where no thief approacheth, neither moth corrupteth."[c]

Jesus also told us where to invest. In fact, He was so excited about this investment opportunity that He said it is even worth selling things you own to invest more! He encouraged us to invest our treasures, our resources of time and money, someplace where they will not rust, rot, or be stolen. Jesus said the safest place for our treasure is in heaven. The truth of Jesus' teaching is evident. Where else can you deposit your treasure that will ensure eternal benefits? Every other investment will either mold, rust, or be left behind when you die. God intends that we earn, that we invest in the future, and that we deposit our investments with Him for safekeeping.

Hearts and Treasures

Let's look at another truth Jesus shared. He went on to say, "For where your treasure is, there will your heart be also."[d]

Pay close attention to His words here. These familiar words have the potential to change your life. Jesus was saying that your heart will follow your treasure. In fact, He said your treasure and your heart will be in the same place.

I clearly remember buying my first car. It took all the money I had in the bank and some additional money I (foolishly) borrowed. I effectively deposited all of my monetary treasure in this vehicle. Suddenly THE CAR consumed my thoughts. THE CAR was polished and pampered. Although I would have probably denied it at the time, my heart was wrapped around THE CAR. I had invested treasure there, and my heart had followed it.

This truth Jesus taught regarding your heart and your treasure may

[c]Luke 12:33
[d]Matthew 6:21

seem negative. But there are a couple of blessings you should consider. Because your heart automatically follows your treasure, you can quite easily determine where your heart is. Just locate your treasure. Find out where your money, time, and energy tend to go. If your discretionary (extra) money seems to end up in the local sporting goods store, you can be sure sporting goods have a part of your heart.

> YOU CAN QUITE EASILY DETERMINE WHERE YOUR HEART IS. JUST LOCATE YOUR TREASURE.

Our Hearts Move

But another truth should be an encouragement to the young man or woman who is serious about following the Lord. Since we know that our hearts follow our treasure, we have the ability to control where our heart goes. We spend a lot of time asking for revival and requesting God to change our hearts. We pray prayers such as, "Lord, give me a heart that loves you more." Or, "Lord, help me to love the things you love." Charles Wesley said it like this in a song we love to sing:

O for a heart to praise my God,
A heart from sin set free,
A heart that always feels Thy blood
So freely shed for me.

These prayers and songs are good requests. We want hearts that will more fully love our Lord, and I believe our Father honors these prayers.

But God has already given us the ability to move our hearts toward Him. Think of Jesus' teaching as a tremendous opportunity. Every time you invest in the Kingdom of Jesus Christ with pure motives, your heart moves a little closer to God. Each time you give to the poor, help someone who is struggling, or even give a cup of cold water in the name of Jesus, your heart moves closer to Him.

Remember this as you make decisions regarding your time and money. With each decision, regardless of how small, your heart is moving either closer to or farther from the Kingdom of God. Take some time to grasp the magnitude of this truth. When you choose to spend "your" money on an earthly treasure, your heart moves a little farther from God. But when you invest in the Kingdom of God by helping the poor or promoting the Kingdom, your heart moves closer to God.

> WITH EACH DECISION, REGARDLESS OF HOW SMALL, YOUR HEART IS MOVING EITHER CLOSER TO OR FARTHER FROM THE KINGDOM OF GOD.

Most of us can identify with this. If you help sponsor a child in Africa, a part of your heart moves there. You notice current events in the newspaper regarding Africa and pray for the people there. Or if you have been quietly helping a widow in your congregation, you find your thoughts turning toward her. Suddenly you are more interested in her welfare and how her life is going. You find yourself hurting when she hurts and desiring to help her more.

What you are experiencing is simply the reality of this truth Jesus taught. Where your treasure is, there your heart will be. This is why it is so important to closely examine where your treasure is going. It is also why every purchase can be a spiritual decision. God has given us an amazing opportunity! Simply by choosing to invest in the Kingdom, we can draw closer to Him!

Conclusion

We all make many decisions every day, and as we have seen in Jesus' teachings, these little choices have a profound effect on our spiritual lives. If you establish your value system from the world around you, it is easy to believe that your use of money doesn't matter. You will find yourself thinking thoughts like, *Why does it really matter what I do with my money? It's really not that big of a deal.*

But if you are using Jesus' teachings to develop a Biblical value system, you will find yourself wanting to invest as much as possible in the Kingdom. His teachings remind us that life is short and that we have a wonderful opportunity each day. Every day my heart can draw closer to God as I use resources correctly. So ask yourself: Are the things I am investing my time, money, and energy into a good investment? Or are they heading for the junkyard?

For Further Reflection

1. Make a list of things we pursue that will end up in the junkyard. Make another list of ways we can invest in wealth that will last.

2. Make a list of items that have little or no use, yet are perceived to be valuable because of public opinion.

3. Share some examples of times your heart has followed your treasure—maybe a time you invested time or money in something and then found your thoughts beginning to go there.

4. What are some steps we can take to move our hearts toward the Kingdom of God?

A Steward? What's That? | 7

WHEN I DIE, IF I LEAVE BEHIND ME TEN POUNDS . . . YOU AND ALL MANKIND MAY BEAR WITNESS AGAINST ME, THAT I HAVE LIVED AND DIED A THIEF AND A ROBBER.

—JOHN WESLEY

There's a story of two teenage country boys who were standing out behind the barn talking one day.

"Bob," said Billy, "if you had a million dollars, would you give me half of it?"

"Of course I would," replied Bob. "You know I would share with you."

"What if you had ten thousand dollars? Would you give me half of that?"

"Of course," Bob replied instantly. "We've been friends since we were little."

"Well," said Billy, scratching his chin, "if you had two pigs, would you give me one?"

"That's not fair!" shouted Bob. "You know I have two pigs!"

Often young people fall into the trap that Bob fell into. It is easy to talk of how I would like to give to the Lord in the future. It is not difficult to imagine becoming prosperous in a business and then giving lots of money to help those in need. But sometimes we fail to grasp the concept of stewardship where we are right now.

What Is Stewardship?

Some time ago I was asked to take a trip for a non-profit organization. I had never before taken a trip where the expenses were paid by someone else, so they told me how to keep track of my costs and submit my expenses for reimbursement.

It seemed as though all the hotels in that city were expensive. That first night I couldn't find a hotel with a reasonable rate, and I found myself worrying about the expense. I pictured turning in the cost to the organization and then receiving a phone call asking why I had spent so much. The organization was known for frugality and kept its expenses as low as possible. People who donated money probably would not be pleased if they found out their money was spent on expensive hotels. The directors had not told me how much to spend. They had simply trusted me to use good judgment.

You see, I was a steward. I was authorized to spend money that belonged to the organization. Others looking on at the hotel counter would have assumed I was spending my own money. But I knew I would need to give an account later for how I spent it. I felt a certain weight of responsibility.

Later as I reflected on what I felt, I realized with shame that I should have felt that same accountability to the Lord years before. I had stood at hotel counters many times thinking only how much it would cost me. I hadn't really been thinking like a steward. I had been viewing the money I was spending as mine. Now I found myself more concerned about this organization's opinion of me than I had been before about God's.

During my teenage years I worked for my father in a small construction company. I often went to the lumberyard to get supplies. Many items on display would have been nice to own. New hammers, fancy tool belts, and other miscellaneous items were tempting to a young man. My father had a charge account at the lumberyard, and it would have been easy for me to purchase a few of these items and put them on his account.

But doing this never really crossed my mind. I knew at the end of the month my father would receive a statement from the lumberyard showing everything that had been purchased. I knew Father would not be pleased to see these items on the bill. I was just a steward for my father. The charge account and the money to pay the bill were his, not mine. Because of this, I was authorized to buy only those things my father wanted me to purchase.

A steward is a representative for the owner. Getting a proper understanding of this truth while you are young can be a blessing all through life. If you are an owner, you are entitled to spend your money however you wish. It is yours to spend. But if you are a steward, then you are in control of things that someone else owns. With stewardship comes responsibility. Stewardship in the Christian life is not just a wonderful idea or something nice to discuss when studying the Bible with friends. It's a way of life and a reality for Kingdom believers who are serious about serving the Lord and building His Kingdom.

STEWARDSHIP . . . IS NOT JUST A WONDERFUL IDEA OR SOMETHING NICE TO DISCUSS WHEN STUDYING THE BIBLE WITH FRIENDS. IT'S A WAY OF LIFE.

It is tempting to view stewardship as a principle that applies only to finances, but Kingdom stewardship goes much deeper than that. Jesus said, "For unto whomsoever much is given, of him shall be much required."[a] What have you been given? Take an inventory of your life and analyze the assets God has given you.

Were you born into a godly home? That is an incredible asset. It is estimated that as many as three billion people have never even heard the name of Jesus,[1] and many others have heard the Good News but have never seen it lived out. If you have lived in a Christian home, you have been given something of amazing value.

Or what about plenty of food? Americans seem obsessed with eating. We chase all the latest flavors, restaurants, and diet plans. Sometimes it seems that our lives revolve around our stomachs. In spite of this preoccupation with eating, food costs consume only a tiny portion of our income. But while all this is going on, an estimated 925 million people in the world struggle with malnutrition. This means that one in seven people are hungry, and this percentage continues to climb.

If you can attend a church meeting without fear of harassment, arrest, torture, or death, be thankful. Thousands are killed each year just for being Christians.[2] If you have been raised with a father in the

[a]Luke 12:48

home, you should be thanking the Lord daily. Four out of ten children in America do not have this privilege.[3]

We read these statistics, yet the reality of how blessed most of us are is difficult to comprehend. We spend a lot of time comparing ourselves with our affluent neighbors, and because of this we don't always feel very well off. But God views us from a global perspective, and all of us are blessed.

How about personal talents and abilities? God said that a steward is responsible and must give an account for his use of the assets he has been given. Do you have any God-given abilities? Are you capable of writing letters of encouragement, singing to lift the spirits in a rest home, or even giving a smile while walking down the street? These abilities are investments that God has made in you, and God expects return on His investment.

What about time? Do you have time that is not allocated for something? What do you do when you have a day, a few hours, or even just a few minutes to spare? Sometimes we think that someone who runs frantically from one important project to another must be using his time well. But good time management is not the speed at which one works as much as the proper use of time. Time is an asset God gives us, and sometimes we forget how valuable it is. Try to identify time wasters in your life. It may be empty reading material, frivolous games, or certain types of technology. Imagine the good that could be accomplished in your community if you used that time for the Kingdom.

All of these resources—a godly heritage, possessions, abilities, and time itself—are gifts from God. You may have more or less than your neighbor, but whatever you have has been given by God for a purpose.

When we believe in the Lord Jesus and become His followers, every resource we previously thought of as ours is given back to Him. This principle was clear to the early church. Notice these words in the beginning of Acts as the writer describes the change in those first believers: "And the multitude of them that believed were of one heart and of one soul: neither said any of them that ought of the things which he possessed was his own."[b]

[b]Acts 4:32

Can you grasp the profound message in this verse? These people, just the day before, knew what they owned. Some of them were probably very wealthy. But immediately following their conversion, they did not call anything their own. They willingly gave up the right of ownership. I don't read of the apostles telling the multitude they had to do this. I believe it is simply the normal response when a man or woman really meets the Lord. Some of these men may have been worth millions of dollars in our economy. But who wants a million dollars when you can have the Lord? What is that in comparison to being a son or daughter of the King of the universe Himself?

> WHO WANTS A MILLION DOLLARS WHEN YOU CAN HAVE THE LORD?

The Apostle Paul described it like this to the church at Corinth: "What? Know ye not that your body is the temple of the Holy Ghost which is in you, which ye have of God, and ye are not your own? For ye are bought with a price: therefore glorify God in your body, and in your spirit, which are God's."[c] The truth contained in this verse should have a great effect on how we use what God has given us. Paul is reiterating the message of stewardship to the wealthy church at Corinth, and these words have a powerful message for us today as well. If you are in Christ and have committed your life to Him, He now owns everything you have—the money in your bank account, the cash in your wallet, even your abilities, vehicles, and time. They are all His.

The question we are left with then is this: "Lord, what should I be doing with your resources?" In the past we may have wondered, "What do I want to do with my time today?" We now ask, "How does God want me to spend His time today?"

Years ago I worked on a construction project for a very wealthy man. This man counted his net worth in billions of dollars, and he had a steward. Since this very rich man had several homes and was rarely available when construction decisions needed to be made, the steward was in charge of making project decisions. The wealthy owner

[c] 1 Corinthians 6:19, 20

was difficult to get along with, and I always felt a little sorry for the steward. Day after day we came to the steward with questions and problems. He couldn't avoid the issues. He had to make decisions, or the project would have stopped.

We were working inside the wealthy man's home, so each choice the steward made would be obvious to the owner when he returned. I marveled at the way the steward was able to make these decisions. I finally concluded there was only one way he could do this. He had made knowing the mind of his master a priority. The steward had observed which colors his master liked and what kinds of wood he preferred. He had studied his likes and dislikes until he could be fairly certain what choice his master would make in any given situation.

Conclusion

We have been called to be stewards in the Kingdom of God. We have willingly given up every right to the resources we once thought of as ours. Our goal now is to use those resources as He would want us to use them. Whether it is our money or our time, we desire that it would be used to His glory and in ways that would please Him.

So how can we know how He wants these resources used? By becoming students of the mind of our Master. We need to spend time in His Word learning His desires. We need to spend time in prayer, intently listening for His Spirit to speak. Sometimes we receive new insight into our Master's wishes from other faithful followers.

> STUDY THE MIND OF THE MASTER, UNTIL THE MASTER HIMSELF BECOMES MASTER OF YOUR MIND.

Our goal is to study the mind of the Master, until the Master Himself becomes Master of our mind. Only then can we really be profitable stewards, and only then will we find "our" resources beginning to flow where He would want them.

For Further Reflection

1. Share a time when you forgot that you were a steward and made a decision you later regretted.

2. Make a list of time wasters that young people tend to become involved in.

3. Create another list of activities you could replace time wasters with that would bless the Kingdom.

4. Since we are stewards, discuss the importance of knowing what our Lord wants us to do with His goods.

5. What are some practical steps we can take to help us know the mind of our Master?

Developing a Kingdom-Focused Vision 8

NO ONE PLANS TO FAIL,
BUT MANY HAVE FAILED TO PLAN.

I clearly remember those exciting teenage years. I was given opportunity to begin making my own choices. My parents had seemed so restrictive while I was growing up, and I found myself longing for freedom. Now I had a good job with few expenses. Consequently, I had more money at my disposal than I ever had before. Life looked good. But even though my expenses were minimal since I was living at home, money did not stay in my pocket long. There were always things calling for cash, and it was difficult to save.

Finally I purchased my first car. There was nothing as exciting as having my own set of wheels. Life really seemed good now. Everything was so accessible, and I felt independent and free. I still had rules to follow, restrictions on evenings away from home, and a curfew to obey, but something about having my own car thrilled my teenage heart.

But my car brought something else. Suddenly I found it even harder to save money. Now there were payments to make, monthly insurance bills to pay, and fuel to buy. Besides these necessary costs, I found myself buying little gadgets to dress up my car. Accessory catalogs advertised an endless array of options. I found myself poring through these catalogs and frequently purchasing small items to enhance my driving experience.

Sports and hobbies were also a big part of my life. Baseball gloves, hunting equipment, fishing tackle, and other miscellaneous sporting gear consumed much of my extra cash. The list of items I "needed" seemed endless. To top it all off, I wanted to learn to fly. Few passions consume cash like aviation, but the fact that I had a good job and few expenses made all this possible.

Then came courtship. As my interest in my future wife increased, I found my interest in all these other activities decreasing. My focus shifted. As our relationship became more serious, I began to think about the financial realities of marriage. Life began to take on a more sober tone. Saving money became more important to me, and the trinkets and pastimes I had been pursuing lost their pull.

If Only . . .

I have watched young-married couples look back over their teenage years with regret. Life just looks different when the bills are piling up, and yet you can remember how freely you spent money just a few years earlier. I remember working with one young couple who was having difficulty with their finances. As we discussed ways they could shave a few dollars here and there to meet their expenses, the wife gazed blankly out my office window at the two vehicles she and her husband had arrived in. "If only," she said, "we wouldn't have bought such nice cars. We had so much extra money back then, but now we don't even have enough to cover necessities." In referring to "back then," she was looking back only a couple of years. Both of them had borrowed to purchase their vehicles. Now the loans were more than the value of the vehicles, and they were having trouble making payments. Life had changed quickly for that young couple. Suddenly, having a nice vehicle was not so important; paying the rent was.

Our lives change. Things that at one point seem very important lose their value. Other items that seemed insignificant suddenly become vital. It is important to establish a Kingdom-focused vision in our youth. Often poor choices made while we are young follow us as we mature. Debt acquired in our youth follows us and keeps us from being able to share with others as we would like.

In this chapter we want to watch a hypothetical young man's life and his use of discretionary income through his early adult years. Discretionary income is money not needed for necessities—the money left over after we have purchased all the items needed for survival.

As we observe this young man's financial life, try to gain some insight into the importance of having a clear and focused vision during these early years. Picture in your mind how these years can be used to bless the Kingdom and develop life patterns that can bless you for years to come. This period of time will greatly impact the rest of your life.

John's Income

As we walk through this account, refer to the graph that follows. The line at the top of the gray area represents John's income, and the black area represents John's necessary expenses. John lived with his parents during these years, so his expenses were minimal. Though many youth help support their families with their incomes, John's money was his own to spend.

First, let's look at John's income. John grew up in a small community, and when he was fifteen he began working during the summer for a local company we will call Quality Electrical. As you can see on the chart, he earned about $3,000 that first summer. But as the years rolled by, John brought more money home. He became more valuable to his employer, and his wages continued to increase. During those first few years while John was still in school, he could only work during the summers and after school. But when he turned eighteen and his schooling was finished, John was able to work full time at Quality Electrical. Consequently, his wages increased dramatically, and by

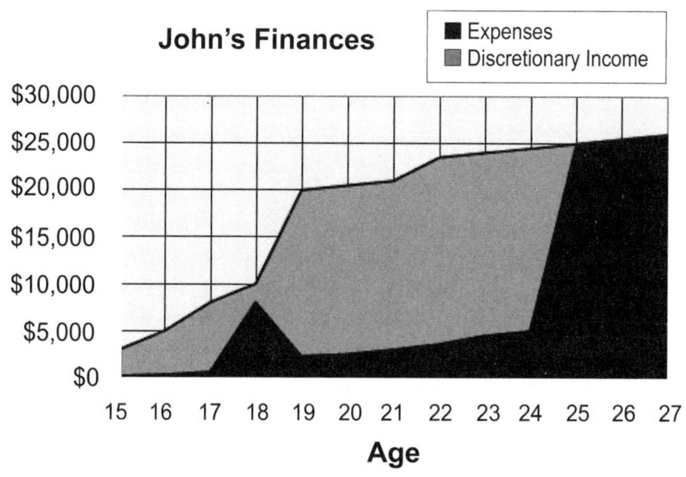

the time John was nineteen he was earning almost $20,000 a year. At twenty-two, John was made foreman of a crew. With this new and increased responsibility came a pay increase, and as you can see on the chart, his income continued to climb. By the time he was twenty-five, he was earning about $25,000 a year.

John's Expenses

Now let's follow John's expenses during this time, represented on the chart by the black area. When we speak of expenses in this illustration, we are referring to necessary costs. As we mentioned earlier, John was living with his parents those first few years, so he did not have many necessary expenses, just some electrical tools for his job and a few miscellaneous items along the way.

When he was seventeen, John's total expenses were less than $1,000 a year. When John was eighteen, his employer asked him to provide his own transportation to the jobsite each day, so John was required to purchase a vehicle. He found an older pickup that seemed to be in good repair, and he was able to purchase it for $7,500. As you can see on the chart, this purchase made an impact on his expenses for the next few years. Now he had to pay for insurance, occasional repairs as the truck aged, and of course, fuel. By the time John was twenty-four, his annual expenses had climbed to about $5,000 a year.

When John was twenty-three, he became interested in a young girl in his congregation named Mary. This relationship blossomed, and when John was almost twenty-five, he married her. This brought a dramatic change to his financial life. Suddenly a host of items cried out for money. Rent, groceries, utilities, and medical bills all had to be paid. All of these expenses, which John's parents had been taking care of, now became John's responsibility. John's expenses increased almost $20,000 in one year.

But we want to leave the expenses and income for a while and look at the area in between. This area, which is gray on the graph, represents the discretionary income throughout John's early life. Look back at the graph again and notice how much discretionary money went through John's hands during those years. If you add up all of John's discretionary income from the time he was fifteen until he was married, you will find it comes to around $130,000.

One Hundred Thirty Thousand Dollars!

Now that is an amazing amount of money, especially since the figures in this study are very conservative. We are assuming that John was making only $10 an hour when he was twenty years old, and many young men are making much more than this. But remember, our goal here is to get a picture of how these early years can be used to bless the Kingdom and prepare us for future life. To do this, let's back up and look at what John might have done with all this money.

Where Did All That Money Go?

You will notice that the study above said nothing regarding how John used this $130,000. As I have worked with a few young people and tried to help them with their finances, I have been amazed how much money they can spend in just a few years. Many have little to show for all the money they have earned. Let's take a look at where John's discretionary money could have gone.

Let's imagine that John had a cell phone. Most other young people had one, so peer pressure was strong. At first the phone plan did not look that expensive, but by the time he paid for all the extras he wanted, then paid the taxes and fees that accompanied the plan, it usually cost John about $85 a month. And then there were food costs. The friends he was with made several trips to town each week, and of course the thing to do was go out to eat. After all, who wants to eat at home all the time? So John ended up spending around $35 a week at restaurants.

In addition to these expenses, John made another decision when he was twenty that had a major impact on his financial situation. He decided he did not want to drive an older pickup around, so he bought a new car. The payments on this car, with the added insurance, amounted to about $400 a month, but this did not worry John too much, since many of his friends were paying even more.

Now let's suppose that John, like most boys, enjoyed some outdoor recreation. He liked to hunt and fish, and let's say that with all the associated equipment, fees, magazine subscriptions, and other costs, John spent around $1,200 each year on his hobbies.

Clothing also consumed a sizable chunk of John's income. His friends often changed their wardrobes, and it became a habit to stop by the mall or the local shopping center to see what was new.

And finally, miscellaneous expenses seemed to pop up everywhere—little items like car magazines, haircuts, and the occasional recreational trip. None of these expenses seemed very great in themselves, but it was amazing how fast a couple hundred dollars slipped through John's hands.

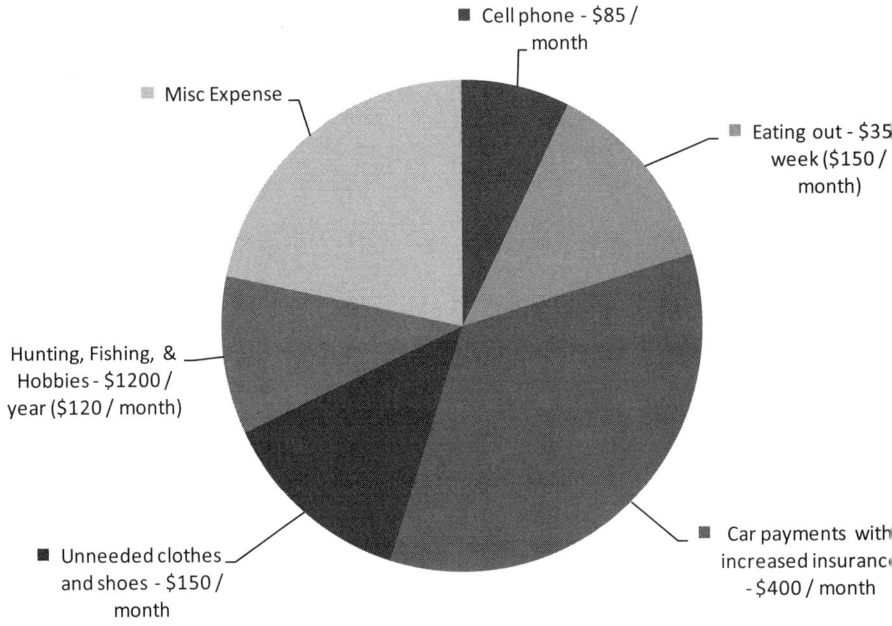

Now this scenario may seem extreme. Maybe you cannot imagine how someone could actually spend $150 on unneeded clothing, or average $200 on miscellaneous expenses. But my experience in dealing with young people who have no plan or long-term vision for their finances is that they spend far more than they realize.

In fact, this example is unfortunately very common. Where there is no vision, there is no purpose, and when we lack purpose, we rarely plan. Consequently, as the saying goes, "Failing to plan is planning to fail." In the scenario above, John would have consumed almost all of his discretionary income during this ten-year period. When he married at the age of twenty-four, he would have had almost nothing to start a home with.

But what could John's life have been like? Imagine how a young couple could use a hundred thousand dollars when first married. Or think about how many people with real needs John could have helped along the way.

A Rare Opportunity

This period of time, early in life, is very important. Few of us understand just how important until it is past. We are given a rare opportunity in our youth. Go back briefly to the discretionary income graph. Notice again how much discretionary income was available before John married and how dramatically this changed after marriage. Most young married couples have very little, if any, extra income. As children come and expenses continue to increase, most people do not see a significant amount of discretionary income for many years.

Conclusion

Perhaps all of this seems insignificant to you right now. Maybe all that seems important to you is acceptance by your peers and having a good time with your friends. That is understandable, and most of us who are older can relate. But the future does finally become reality. This lesson is not intended to shame you if you have spent money on unneeded clothing or unnecessary technology. All of us have made poor choices. But it is important to understand the consequences of failing to plan.

Imagine what it would be like to be twenty-five years old and wish you could back up and use your money differently. Even if you have no interest in settling down and establishing a family at this point, you will never regret taking the time to plan your use of money. This is even more important if you have a serious desire to develop a Kingdom vision. Start planning now while you are young if you really want to serve the Lord Jesus with every part of your life.

For Further Reflection

1. Imagine you are John's parents. How could you have helped him through this time of his life?

2. Discuss some practical steps John could have taken in his youth to organize his discretionary income.

3. Make a list of activities and purchases that seem exciting and important while we are young, yet might seem frivolous and wasteful when we are older and looking back.

4. Looking at John's life, discuss how his discretionary money could have been used. What percentage should youth give? What percentage should be saved?

Whose Kingdom Are You Building? 9

THE REAL MEASURE OF OUR WEALTH IS HOW MUCH WE'D BE WORTH IF WE LOST ALL OUR MONEY.
—**JOHN HENRY JOWETT**

When I was a young man, I came home one evening and found a salesman for a large mutual fund company sitting in our living room talking to my parents. The salesman was just finishing his presentation, so he decided to see if he could interest me in his investment program.

He began by asking my age. I told him I was nineteen, and he pulled out some charts and began explaining what a wonderful opportunity I had at my age. He could tell I enjoyed finance, so he proceeded to show me what a small investment each month could do over a long period of time. The figures he gave me were amazing.

All I had to do was deposit $25 each week in the mutual fund he was marketing. By the time I was sixty-five and ready to retire, he explained, I would have over $1,100,000 in my account. With that much money, I could do whatever I wanted. And the best part, he added, was that most of it would be from the income of stocks and bonds within the fund. In fact, I would only have put in about $55,000 of my own money during those years, and the rest would have come from income on my investment.

Imagine the Possibilities!

I remember getting out my calculator and doing the math. This was amazing! Of course, much of this was based on the stock market, and no one really knew where that was going. But the basic premise this salesman presented was correct. Compound interest has been called the eighth wonder of the world, and as a teenager I was enthralled with this concept. If you invest over a long enough period of time, a small investment will multiply tremendously and generate a large sum in the end.

I didn't take that salesman's advice. While the concept intrigued me, there were a lot of other things to do with $25 each week.

Looking back, I see the salesman was right. Even though there have been many ups and downs in the financial markets in the intervening years, if I had started putting $25 each week into his mutual fund, I would be well on my way to having a million dollars in my account by the time I am sixty-five.

Recently I listened to a Christian financial speaker give almost the same presentation. "Just be patient and keep investing," he instructed. "By the time you are ready for retirement, you will have enough money in your account to live comfortably through your retirement years."

All of this is true. But it is imperative before we go very far that we decide which kingdom we are trying to build.

The Wise Man Who Was a Fool

The Bible tells of a man we refer to as the rich fool. But I doubt his neighbors thought of him as a fool. I suspect he was regarded as a wise man in his community. I imagine people came to him when they had questions regarding finance or farming. Jesus even revealed this man's thoughts. This man was thinking smart thoughts. He saw that the harvest was greater than his ability to store, so he decided to save the extra for the future. Nothing stupid about this man. He knew how to plan ahead. He knew that not every year would be a bumper year and he should be setting something aside for the future. In fact, as I read this account, it sounds amazingly similar to the teaching I hear from "Christian" financial teachers today. If Jesus had not called this man a fool, we would

"IF JESUS HAD NOT CALLED THIS MAN A FOOL, WE WOULD PROBABLY BE USING HIM AS AN EXAMPLE OF WISE INVESTING."

probably be using him as an example of wise investing. We would have seminars and charts on the wall telling about this man's wisdom.

But Jesus called him a fool, and I would encourage you to spend time meditating on the twelfth chapter of Luke to understand why. Jesus concluded this account by saying, "So is he that layeth up treasure for himself, and is not rich toward God."[a] Now, what does that mean? What does it mean to have treasure for myself, yet not be rich toward God? We know how a man can be rich on earth, but how can a man be rich toward God? If you ask most Christian financial teachers today, they will say something like this: "Being rich toward God just means believing on Him and accepting what He has done for you." But is a mental assent to what Jesus did on the cross all that Jesus was speaking of?

The reason it is important to read this entire twelfth chapter of Luke is that Jesus did not leave us without an answer to this question. Immediately following this account of the rich fool, Jesus tells us how much time we should spend worrying about the future, how much regard we should give to food and clothing, and exactly how to be rich toward God.

How to Really Be Rich

"Sell that ye have," Jesus said, "and give alms; provide for yourselves bags which wax not old, a treasure in the heavens that faileth not, where no thief approacheth, neither moth corrupteth. For where your treasure is, there will your heart be also."[b]

> WE COULD SAY THE RICH FOOL WAS GOOD AT INVESTING; HE WAS JUST INVESTING IN THE WRONG KINGDOM.

Jesus says that giving to those in need is how we become rich toward God. Jesus was not condemning investing. Actually, he commands it. But there are different ways to invest and different places to store our investments. We can summarize the lesson we get from the man Jesus called a fool in this way: He was a wise

[a]Luke 12:21
[b]Luke 12:33, 34

earthly investor but a poor heavenly one. Or we could say he was good at investing; he was just investing in the wrong kingdom.

The Kingdom of Self Versus the Kingdom of God

We come into this world as completely self-centered individuals. As infants, we are usually complaining a few seconds after we are born. We cry if we are hungry, holler if someone is not paying attention to us, or fuss if too many people do. Everything that happens is gauged by how it affects us. As we grow older, we learn how to mask our self-centeredness. We learn to appear loving while really trying to get our own way. We find that we can get more of what we want by being kind. In short, we find ourselves developing a little kingdom we will call the kingdom of self.

The kingdom of self is very much like the kingdoms of this world. We look out for our own interests, just as natural kingdoms do. We are ready to defend ourselves, just as the country where we live does. We want to look good, have people admire us, and be happy. That is the kingdom of self.

But Jesus compares the kingdom of self with the Kingdom of God and tries to show us the foolishness of focusing on the kingdom of self. He talks about our preoccupation with food, clothing, and housing. These things all concern the kingdom of self. A man who is focused on the kingdom of self finds his thoughts revolving around these topics. Then, after addressing our tendency to focus on the kingdom of self, Jesus says this: "But rather seek ye the kingdom of God."[c] God knows we need food, clothes, and shelter. But He asks us to take our focus off all these things and focus instead on the Kingdom of God. Jesus is asking for a conscious decision. He is asking us to stop building one kingdom and start building another.

Whose Kingdom Are You Building?

I think it not only a fair question, but also a very important one. Whose kingdom are you building? Do you find your thoughts circling around food, clothes, and material things, or is your primary interest

[c] Luke 12:31

and concern the Kingdom of God? Make no mistake about it. You cannot build both kingdoms at the same time with the same money. The one kingdom calls for you to save and accumulate, the other tells you to share and distribute.

The kingdom of self will tell you to protect yourself; the Kingdom of God will encourage you to trust in Him.

> "YOU CANNOT BUILD BOTH KINGDOMS AT THE SAME TIME WITH THE SAME MONEY."

I believe it is extremely important early in your Christian life to get a clear picture of what it means to build the Kingdom of God. This overriding vision will help you deal with the smaller questions that come from day to day.

Conclusion

Let's go back to the salesman who was promoting the investment plan. For only $25 each week I could be prepared for retirement. With over a million dollars in the bank, I could choose just how I wanted to spend my golden years. I could eat out occasionally, take a trip now and then, and enjoy what I had accumulated. That sounds really nice, and these types of investments are available to you today. But how do you know whether or not this is something you should do?

To help solve this dilemma, spend some time examining the proposal. Which kingdom is the voice coming from? Is it coming from the kingdom of self or the Kingdom of God? Sometimes this will take some thought and prayer to discern. But take these types of questions to the Lord and view them in the light of Jesus' words. Avoid asking, "What is wrong with it?" If you are truly focused on the Kingdom of God, you will find yourself asking other kinds of questions—questions such as: What could $25 each week do in the Kingdom of God? If I would invest just $25 each week to help feed the hungry, print Bibles for those who cannot buy them, or sponsor a child and help him learn to read, what would happen? How much would that investment grow over time? These questions come from the very heart of God.

For Further Reflection

1. Using the twelfth chapter of Luke as a reference, how is it possible to be rich toward God?

2. Make a list and discuss some ways we can know whose kingdom we are building.

3. What are some steps we can take to ensure we are listening to the Lord and not to our selfish desires?

4. List ways we can use the treasure, time, and talents God gives us for selfish pursuits. Make a corresponding list of ways these resources could be used for the Kingdom.

Putting Your Vision Into Action | 10

NOW THEREFORE PERFORM THE DOING OF IT; THAT AS THERE WAS A READINESS TO WILL, SO THERE MAY BE A PERFORMANCE ALSO.
2 CORINTHIANS 8:11

Most of us like to read the book of Acts. The accounts of those early believers inspire us. From the day of Pentecost in the beginning to Paul being shipwrecked at the end, something is always happening. Isn't that what we like about the book? Acts doesn't just tell us, it shows us! It's not called the Intentions of the Apostles; it is the Acts of the Apostles.

In the last chapter we talked about the importance of having a Kingdom vision. We considered some of the teachings of Jesus and what He said about money. We looked at the difference between focusing on the kingdom of self and building the Kingdom of God. In the next few chapters we want to look at implementing our vision.

It is wonderful to have a vision for building the Kingdom of God, but how can we actually carry it out? What steps can we take with our finances to surrender our lives more completely to Jesus? And even more specifically, what can you do while you are young to ensure that Kingdom building becomes a reality in every part of your life?

- **Diligence and discipline.** We want to look at the importance of developing personal diligence and discipline in our lives. Living for the Kingdom will be a battle. Choosing to commit your finances to the Lord Jesus will not be easy. You will be going against the flow of society. You will be opposed by your culture and possibly even your friends. It is important to understand and expect this.

- **Budgeting.** We will also look briefly at how a budget can help us funnel more of our resources toward the Kingdom. Perhaps you have tried budgeting in the past and finally given up. We want to look at how an overriding goal of blessing others and living for Jesus can help you stay focused and assist you in keeping your finances on track.

- **Choosing a career.** How are you to decide what to do for a living? Maybe your father has always farmed; should you keep on farming? Does it really matter what your occupation is? Should you be concerned about how much income a job brings in? We want to address some of these questions and consider what kind of an impact your occupation can have on your life. Some careers can be helpful to your goal of living for the Lord, and other occupations can make Kingdom living more difficult.

- **Money and marriage.** If you feel that the Lord is calling you to marriage, how much regard should you give to your prospective spouse's view of money? Should you talk about money and possessions before marriage? What about debt? Does your future partner's view on debt really matter? Should you talk about renting a house versus buying one? How about saving for retirement? Is that something you want to do? Does your prospective spouse agree? These are good questions, and we want to find some answers.

- **Single life—serving the Lord without distraction.** Not everyone is called to marriage. Can unmarried individuals really be useful in the Kingdom? What special roles can they play in the body of Christ that someone with a spouse or children cannot? We want to look at some wonderful opportunities available to singles and some of the advantages they possess.

- **Investing in the Kingdom.** If you follow the teachings of Jesus literally, how much of your income should you give?

Is 10 percent required? Is 10 percent enough? And where should you give?

Putting Your Vision Into Action

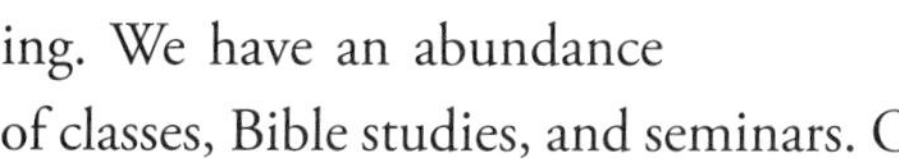

All of these areas are significant, but before we address them individually, let's look at the importance of action in our lives. One of the reasons we are drawn to the book of Acts is because such activity is lacking in "Christianity" today. There is no shortage of teaching. We have an abundance of classes, Bible studies, and seminars. Our bookstores are full, our stacks of reading material higher than we can get through, and our Sunday services filled with good messages telling us how to live the Christian life. Our mailboxes can be filled with religious magazines, newsletters, and periodicals.

Technology allows us access to even more information. Many people spend hours every day listening to spiritual messages, Gospel music, and even the Word of God itself. Thousands of websites offer religious teaching, webinars to help believers find victory in Christ, and chat rooms where you can ask Scriptural questions and get answers from other serious seekers around the globe. While much of this teaching may be erroneous, some of it is very good. In our day there is no excuse for ignorance. We are inundated with teaching and information.

Stop for just a moment and compare our situation with that of believers in the book of Acts. How much teaching material did they have? How many seminars did they attend? Many early believers could not even read or write, yet we marvel at their power. Today we regard information as power, but how could those early believers have had so much power while in possession of so little information?

What Happened to the Power?

A story has been told for centuries regarding Thomas Aquinas, an Italian priest in the thirteenth century. The pope was walking through the Vatican one day with Thomas, showing him all the glory of the Roman Catholic Church.

"You see, Thomas," said the pope with pride and great satisfaction, "the church can no longer say with Peter of old, 'Silver and gold have I none.' "

"No," Thomas agreed, "and neither can it say, 'In the name of Jesus . . . , rise up and walk'!"

The church in Thomas's day had great wealth, but no spiritual power. This story of Thomas Aquinas reminds me of our time. We have a wealth of information, but so little power. I wonder if our society in this information age is having a greater effect on us than we realize. We chase the latest books, CDs, and speakers as though we believe more information is what we need. But are we really lacking knowledge? Is our lack of power in the church today due to a lack of information?

Do What You Know

> KNOWLEDGE WITHOUT ACTION IS WORTHLESS.

I do not want to encourage anyone to stop seeking knowledge. God loves to see His children hungry for more knowledge of Him. But knowledge without action is worthless. I want to encourage you to be more active in doing what you already know. Isn't that what inspires us about the early church? They not only had a vision of living for the Kingdom—they did it! They took those basic teachings on how to regard money and possessions and actually lived them out.

I have been ashamed many times as I look at my own life. How many times have I listened to a message or read a convicting writing and been so inspired and convicted of my need to change that I decided to transform some area of my life? I would even get serious enough to pray and ask God to help me in this area. But some time later I would look back with regret and realize nothing had actually changed.

I had become convicted, decided to make a change, and visualized what needed to take place, but the plan had never become reality.

There is something else we should note as we compare our Christian way of life today with the early church. Have you ever noticed what followers of Jesus were called in the book of Acts? In our time we typically call ourselves Christians or believers. But something has changed dramatically since Jesus' time. Followers of Jesus were referred to as Christians only twice and as believers once in the entire book of Acts. But they are referred to as disciples many times. In fact, the word *disciple* is used thirty-one times in Acts.

I believe this change is significant. Today we want to know if a person is a believer or a Christian. Our emphasis is on belief. In the early church the word was disciple, and their emphasis was on following. They patterned their lives after Jesus. They wanted to imitate His life, to walk in His steps, to live as He lived. We have a tendency to reduce Christianity to a system of beliefs. We stress theology and correct doctrine. The early disciples talked about suffering with Him and dying for His name. Theology is important, and what you believe about God is foundational to your Christian walk. But God never intended for theology to be an end in itself.

How Discipleship Affects Finances

So how did being a disciple affect the finances of the early Christians? The change was immediate and obvious. Just a few verses after the Bible tells of three thousand souls being baptized on the day of Pentecost, we read about their money and possessions. Jesus' teaching on finances was radically different from His culture, and as these early disciples started applying what He taught, their lives became radically different too. They didn't just sit around and talk about how it could be possible to have money but not trust in it—they wanted to be like Jesus! They wanted to imitate Him, and their money immediately started to flow toward the poor.

Once again, is this not why we enjoy reading about them? They actually did it! I wonder sometimes what a book describing my life and spiritual experience would be titled. "The Theology of Gary," or maybe,

"What Gary Said He Believed." But, "The Acts of Gary"? How thick would that book be? If you wrote down the changes that following Jesus has made in your finances, how much would you have to write? These earlier followers of Jesus did not just sit and talk; they got up and showed others what God could do. They allowed God to turn their inner belief into outer action.

THESE EARLIER FOLLOWERS OF JESUS ALLOWED GOD TO TURN THEIR INNER BELIEF INTO OUTER ACTION.

Flight Plans

When I was working toward getting my pilot's license, I spent a significant amount of time learning to make and file a flight plan. I took an aviation map and charted out a course. I was taught to begin with a starting point and an estimated time of departure, then draw a line from my departure point to different waypoints along my proposed path, ending at my final destination. I calculated airspeed, cruising altitude, and the estimated time of arrival.

Estimating the time of arrival could be difficult. There were usually crosswinds or headwinds, so I obtained information from the weather service to help estimate these factors. When I had calculated all this, I filed a form with the government. This was designed to help the authorities find me if I did not show up at my destination. After the flight plan was filed, I needed to set the plan in motion. Just before takeoff I called the government authorities, informed them I was ready to leave, and asked them to activate the plan.

Activating Our Vision

A flight plan, like our spiritual vision, is worthless if never activated. We may have spent hours poring over the details of the proposed flight and told others how we planned to fly, but an inactivated plan is worthless. Sometimes I wonder how many of us have well-thought-out Kingdom-building plans that have never been activated. We have spent hours studying the teachings of Jesus. We have been involved in lengthy word studies and can explain in detail the meanings of Greek words. We have compared our Kingdom vision with others and can explain why ours is far superior. But we have never actually activated the plan. We are like a pilot sitting at the end of the runway, rehashing the plan while wasting precious time and fuel.

A young man who lives in a Third World country shared with me that one way to activate a plan is to lay it before the Lord in prayer. He knew of a little indigenous congregation struggling to get going back in the jungle. Moving back in there to help would be difficult, and he found himself wanting to get involved in some other ministry so that when the time came for his church to send someone, he would not be available.

But he chose to lay down his will and ask the Lord to lead, committing himself to go wherever God called. The call came, and he was asked to move. And the experience has been a blessing. He wanted to do something for the Kingdom, but God only spoke after he was willing to lay his life before the Lord and listen to His direction.

Sometimes, in spite of all our talk about wanting to serve the Lord, we subconsciously position ourselves so the Lord cannot use us. By simply over-committing myself financially, I can protect myself from the Lord's call to give. I can feel justified in not stopping to help the person along the road because I have allowed myself to become too busy at work. If God has given you a Kingdom vision, open your heart and your ears to His direction, and then go and do what He asks you to do.

Conclusion

> THE WORLD IS LOOKING FOR DISCIPLES, NOT JUST BELIEVERS.

The pagan and religious cultures surrounding the early church were looking for answers. They had listened to endless debate and philosophy. There were arguments explaining the superiority of one religion or philosophy over another. But why did Christianity alarm religious and government leaders and sweep across the Roman Empire so rapidly? "These people are turning the world upside down!" protested the authorities of the day. What was so different about Christianity?

I think the first answer to this question is simply the resurrection. Christianity had life! But there is something else about those early disciples we would be wise to take note of. They were men and women of action. They were willing to follow Jesus, regardless! Many of them lost their families, their friends, and their finances. They were willing to live radically different lives, and the world sat up and took notice.

Today we wonder why we have no power. We don't understand why our attempts at evangelism yield so few sincere converts. But I believe we, like the early disciples, live in a world that is waiting—looking for men and women who are so dedicated and consecrated to the teachings of Jesus that they are willing to live them out. The world is looking for disciples, not just believers.

For Further Reflection

1. Discuss some differences between the Christianity we observe around us and the Christianity we read about in Acts. What are some reasons for the differences?

2. Do you have any areas in your life where you have felt convicted to make some change, but have never actually changed?

3. Can you think of patterns of life within your youth group where your actions are not consistent with your stated beliefs?

4. If someone asked your neighbors, would they say that you are unaffected by materialism? What would they say the youth in your area are focused on?

Diligence in the Workplace | 11

DILIGENCE OVERCOMES DIFFICULTIES; SLOTH MAKES THEM.
—BENJAMIN FRANKLIN

Being involved in construction, I have had the opportunity to hire and work with young men. Most of them come to work that first day with a determination to do the best they can and a desire to make a good impression on their new boss. But soon the initial enthusiasm wears off and their actual work ethic begins to reveal itself. Some gradually lose their original zeal for the project. They begin to glance more frequently at their watches and become more inclined to stop work and enter into discussion with coworkers. They usually remember when lunchtime starts but have trouble remembering when it ends.

Not Slothful in Business

Others are just the opposite. They always arrive on time, look forward to the day, and maintain interest in the project. One young employee in particular impressed me in this way. I would usually arrive on the jobsite ten or fifteen minutes early to get things ready for the day, and almost every day this young man was already there. I would drive up to a project and see him walking around the building carrying a set of plans, looking at what needed to be accomplished that day. Many times he had a few suggestions, something he had thought about the evening before that might make the day go better. This young man's enthusiasm for the project was contagious. He inspired the other workers, and I found myself asking him questions instead of the foreman.

Few virtues distinguish young men and women as much as their diligence in the workplace. Society around us is becoming more and more "me-focused." Carelessness and negligence are becoming the norm on the jobsite. Because of this, young people who are willing to stand up and do their best in the workplace shine out like beacons. People notice and appreciate these character qualities. Sometimes we forget the amazing potential for outreach that exists on the jobsite.

Mission Motivation

Many young people are interested in reaching out to others. They love to talk about trips they have made to foreign countries or mission trips they would like to be involved in. Even outside the Christian world, the interest in short-term missions has been incredible. *USA Today* described the escalating interest in short-term missions as an "out of control phenomena."[1] Many people view such trips as opportunities to see more of the world while helping others in need. These trips can be eye-opening and have blessed many who have participated.

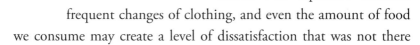

But we also need to understand their limitations. When we go into a foreign setting where the language and culture are drastically different from our own, we are not going to make a great difference in people's lives in two weeks. We may be able to help them with something they could never have accomplished on their own, but most of the benefit will probably be what we take home with us. We also have the potential of doing harm. Our expensive cameras, frequent changes of clothing, and even the amount of food we consume may create a level of dissatisfaction that was not there before we came. This is the reality of some of our short-term missions.

All that being said, I do not believe the answer is to stop short-term mission trips. But we need to understand the downside and take appropriate steps to help rather than hinder the Kingdom in these ventures.

It is easy to think that mission work is something that happens in other countries and forget the great potential in the workplace. We can make a difference for the Kingdom at home, in our communities, and at work.

Mission in the Marketplace

Many years ago my brother and I were working on a small residential remodeling project in California. We had just finished the day's work when a painter named Marvin, who had just started working there, stopped us. He asked a little about our construction business and our families, and then he finally inquired about the issue he was really interested in. Marvin said he had noticed that we dressed a little differently, and he wanted to know more about our religious beliefs. He had grown up with very little spiritual teaching and really had a desire to know truth.

We tried to explain to Marvin the importance of faith in Jesus Christ, and standing there at the back of our work truck, we attempted to share with him our hope of salvation. After a nice discussion, we invited Marvin to come to services with us the next Sunday. He thanked us for the invitation and said, "I really appreciate everything you have said, and it has given me a lot to think about. But I will probably just watch your lives for a while."

Marvin went on to explain how in the past he had asked different people about their faith, and it always sounded so good. But then when he took the time to observe their lives, he was never very impressed. Marvin did not know it, but he was doing exactly what Jesus had said to do. Look for fruit. Make sure what the tree says matches what it produces.

"By Their Fruits Ye Shall Know Them"

I don't think we can comprehend the importance of diligence in the workplace. I love to see young men excited about sharing their faith or distributing good literature to a coworker who needs the Lord. But I have also seen the futility in all of this if the young man lacks diligence in the workplace. If the young believer who wants to proclaim his faith to others exhibits laziness in his work, he will have a difficult time convincing a lost coworker that he has something worth having. The Apostle Paul encouraged the believers in Rome to be "not slothful in business; fervent in spirit; serving the Lord."[a]

> WHAT IF WE VIEWED OUR OCCUPATIONS AS MISSION OUTPOSTS?

One of the ways we fail in diligence is by forgetting the end goal. We tend to think of our occupations only as ways to produce money. The bills keep coming, we keep getting hungry, our car continues to need gas, and the only way to stay ahead of all this is to continue going to work. But what if we viewed our occupations as mission outposts? What would happen if we prayed fervently each day for our coworkers, our employers, and the customers we serve? What if we asked the Lord to bring the needy to us and provide us an opportunity to help them? How would that change our day—and our diligence?

The Apostle Paul, writing to the church at Colosse, encouraged them to be diligent employees. "Servants, obey in all things your masters according to the flesh; not with eyeservice, as menpleasers; but in singleness of heart, fearing God: And whatsoever ye do, do it heartily, as to the Lord, and not unto men; Knowing that of the Lord ye shall receive the reward of the inheritance: for ye serve the Lord Christ."[b]

If you are an employee and are really serious about living for the Kingdom, I encourage you to commit this passage to memory. Tape it on the dash of your vehicle or the bathroom mirror if you need to. I can think of many times when the diligence of a young man or woman has inspired an observer to a closer walk with God. Notice what these verses are saying. Kingdom Christians are not primarily choosing to be diligent for their employer; they are serving the Lord

[a]Romans 12:11
[b]Colossians 3:22-24

Himself! They are looking beyond the fear of getting fired to the reward of faithfully serving the God of the universe!

There's an old story about a traveler who came upon a group of stonemasons working on a large church. The traveler asked each of the masons in turn what they were doing.

The first worker answered, "I am sanding down this block of marble."

The second replied, "I am making a living for my family."

But the third man stopped and said, "I am building a grand cathedral for Almighty God Himself."

Conclusion

In the past few years there has been increasing interest in using the workplace as a mission field. Organizations have sprung up capitalizing on this vision, and seminars and literature are now widely available on this topic. This concept is generally called Business as Missions, and many think it is a new idea. But perhaps we think this concept is new simply because we have ignored basic Scriptural teaching. In our rush to try other quicker and easier methods of reaching out, perhaps we have forgotten the example the early Christians left us. I wonder how many sermons Paul preached while he was busy making tents. I suspect his lessons on diligence became even more powerful as people saw him living it out. Don't you suppose Luke used his experience as a physician in sermons as he explained Paul's analogy of the human body and the body of Christ? Think of the lessons Peter gained in his days as a fisherman. How many illustrations do you suppose he used that were inspired by his nights out in the boat?

We often draw a line between the natural and the spiritual. We begin to think that working at our occupations is some kind of necessary evil—that we would accomplish more in some foreign country passing out tracts and talking to others about Jesus. God does call some to go, and He may call you. But I also believe we are misunderstanding God's will for His Kingdom when we differentiate between mission work and our occupations.

It is possible for a job to be a waste of time. If your goal in being there is self-centered, perhaps you should consider it a waste. If all you are doing there is pursuing your own agenda and wealth, even a good job can be useless to the Lord. But if you are diligent and view your occupation as unto the Lord and not unto men, "ye shall receive the reward of the inheritance: for ye serve the Lord Christ!"[c]

For Further Reflection

1. Can you think of individuals within your community who are known for their diligence in the workplace? Share some examples of things you have seen or heard that tell you they are diligent.

2. Discuss some ways we can bless individuals in Third World settings. How can we do damage? List some ways we can minimize the damage while visiting.

3. Discuss ways we can impact others though our work and hold each other accountable in using the workplace as a mission field.

4. Share ways we can discourage our fellow workers, employers, or customers from seeking the Gospel. How can we encourage them?

[c]Colossians 3:24

Developing Personal Discipline 12

TALENT WITHOUT DISCIPLINE IS LIKE AN OCTOPUS ON ROLLER SKATES. THERE'S PLENTY OF MOVEMENT, BUT YOU NEVER KNOW IF IT'S GOING TO BE FORWARD, BACKWARDS, OR SIDEWAYS.
—H. JACKSON BROWN JR.

I grew up in the Central Valley of California. While many people in our area were quite prosperous, one man and his family were exceptionally wealthy. From childhood I heard stories of how much land this man owned, how vast his financial holdings were, and how large and extravagant his home was.

As I grew older, I realized something else about this man. This man really *wanted* to be rich. Money was extremely important to him. Newspaper write-ups would tell of various lawsuits he was involved in. Someone would threaten his financial empire, and he would strike back through his team of lawyers. Even in his older years, when his life was nearly over and he should have been thinking about preparing for death, he was still chasing wealth. In his eighties, he got into a legal battle with one of his family members. The front page described the nasty brawl that ensued, each brother slandering the other in hopes of hanging on to a little more of the family fortune. This man wanted more and more wealth, and he was determined to get it.

But the account that has always stood out to me in this man's life was how he read the newspapers. Each morning he had one of his employees lay the front pages of the major newspapers on a table for him. This allowed him to briefly scan all the major happenings around the world. Once he had a picture in his mind of what was going on in the world that day, he would head for the office. He was not interested in all the little journalistic details contained in the back pages. He did not want to waste time reading about some famous celebrity's lifestyle. He just wanted the major stories, and primarily the ones that might affect his growing empire.

Those who were knowledgeable about his daily habits said he would never sit down with a newspaper. He knew this could consume valuable time and would not further his goal of gaining wealth. This man had a clear vision. He knew what he wanted and was determined that nothing, not even a newspaper, was going to keep him from achieving his goal.

Dedication and Determination

I have to marvel at this man's dedication and determination. He knew his own weakness and understood that the only way he was going to reach his goal was through personal discipline. He would allow nothing to stand between him and his vision.

Do you have that kind of personal discipline in your pursuit of the Kingdom of God? Are you willing to give up things you enjoy to be a successful warrior for Jesus? How about your use of money? Do you abandon things your flesh craves simply because of your passion for the Kingdom of God? This wealthy man was willing to give up present pleasure and enjoyment to pursue his goal, and his goal was just earthly wealth. Today this man is dead. All that is left is a large tombstone telling how long he lived. His possessions have been distributed to others, and all past effort and personal discipline is of no value to him. He was building the wrong kingdom.

But we can learn from this man's discipline. As you begin your Christian life and start using your resources for the Kingdom of God, you need to understand that it will not be easy. You are not on neutral ground. You are fighting this battle on enemy soil. You will be bombarded with many temptations and powerful allurements. The god of this world will do everything in his power (and he does have power!) to entice you. You will receive pressure from glitzy advertisements, disdainful comments from unbelievers, and even disparaging remarks from professing believers. In addition to this you will need to deal with your own selfish desires. This will require both the Spirit of God and personal discipline.

The Need for Filters

The valley we live in requires irrigation. The fields around us would all be brown if it were not for a network of irrigation ditches throughout the valley. These open ditches are the lifeblood of local agriculture. Water courses through the ditches, into pipes, and eventually out to the field where it is needed. But since these little canals are open, weeds, small sticks, and miscellaneous trash find their way into them. If we allowed debris to continue from the canals into the pipes going out to the fields, we would have a mess. Smaller pipes would become plugged, and given enough time, our whole valley would again become brown, in spite of all the water flowing from the mountain lakes.

The farmers know this, and so they have installed screens in these canals. Just before the water leaves the open ditch and pours into the pipes, it has to go through one of these filters. This ensures that the unwanted debris stays out of the pipes and clean water continues on to where it is needed.

We need filters in our lives as well. So many options flow into our lives, and we need something to determine which options to accept and which to reject. More than just filtering out the evil, we need to make daily choices between things that may not be totally good or bad.

Picture for a moment the canal of options that flows into your life. This canal is full of every choice available to you. It contains all the sports you enjoy, the entertainments that tempt you, and every technological gadget available. It includes the books you want to read, the restaurants you like, and the vehicles you can own. It contains opportunities to help the poor and share the Gospel, and times of prayer and personal devotions.

Every Man Must Choose

Every human of sound mind and body has to have a filter on this canal of options. There isn't even enough time in a lifespan to try every option. The question is not whether or not you are going to make choices, but on what basis you will make them. In other words, what will you use for a filter?

I remember coming face to face with the reality that something I really enjoyed needed to die. I had always wanted to fly. As a small boy riding past the airport, my face would be pressed against the car window. I read about airplanes, asked questions of pilots, and, like many boys, dreamed of flying someday. I imagined the thrill of taking friends on rides and being the envy of my peers. The day finally arrived when I had enough money to begin flying lessons, and I eventually received my pilot's license. Flying was as exciting as I had imagined. You could take off from one location and in just a few minutes land somewhere it would have taken much longer to drive to. Life was great! I had longed for and finally selected something from my canal of options.

The Kingdom Call

But as time went on I began to experience a small inner voice. This voice began to challenge my use of the Lord's resources. To get to the airport in our local town, I had to drive through the low-income area. As I drove past little tumbledown houses and observed the effects of poverty along the streets, I began to wonder. Was flying really where the Lord wanted His resources to be going? Of course, I tried to rationalize my flying. "If these folks would just manage money a little better and hold down a steady job like I do, they wouldn't be in this mess."

But in spite of my arguments, the Lord continued to prod. Finally I knew something had to go. I was going to have to choose between my love of flying and my love for the Kingdom. I wish I could say this was my last battle with my use of resources in the Kingdom, but it wasn't. The battle continues. To this day, more than twenty-five years later, the sound of a small airplane flying overhead pulls at something within me, and I am reminded that the battle is not over yet.

Install a Kingdom Filter

Think about your own life. Do you have competing interests and desires? Is there something in your life that needs to die? Have you installed a Kingdom filter to help you strain out opposing options? If you are really serious about living for the Kingdom of Jesus Christ, you will need to screen your options, and you will need to develop some personal discipline to do this. Let's look at a few of the personal disciplines you will need to successfully install a Kingdom filter.

Read Your Bible

I can think of no better place to start as you develop a Kingdom filter for your life than time in God's Word. Read it, memorize it, discuss it, and you will find the principles of God's Word slowly weaving a powerful filter for your life. Consistent reading is not easy and can be an area of constant frustration to young believers. We are often instructed about the importance of reading the Word daily, yet we frequently become discouraged when trying to put our plans into action. Many times our great and lofty desires to daily commune with the Lord come crashing to the ground when confronted with the reality of the daily battle. Why does this happen? Why do our good intentions vaporize?

Sometimes it may simply be a lack of intense desire. How desperate is your longing for more of God's Word? Is your desire so intense you are willing to give up social events, leisure time, or sleep? Do you honestly believe that your daily survival depends on your personal connection with God? Most of us want to appear spiritual, but we can be amazingly content with our present nearness to (or distance from) God.

Sometimes our Bibles have too much competition. It can be very difficult to maintain a consistent schedule of reading God's Word when surrounded with exciting books and novels. With many of these books, your mind can remain in neutral. The author carries you along from exciting event to exciting event, always tantalizing you and tempting you to continue on. But the Bible is different. It demands that you get involved. It requires you to analyze your life and make hard choices. It isn't always easy to understand and requires time for meditation. If you are going to hear God's voice in His Word, you may need to filter out some of your other reading.

> DO YOU HONESTLY BELIEVE THAT YOUR DAILY SURVIVAL DEPENDS ON YOUR PERSONAL CONNECTION WITH GOD?

Reading God's Word will also require some advance planning. It may necessitate using an alarm clock and planning in advance to give up some social activities. Waiting until morning to decide about spending time with the Lord is a recipe for failure.

> WAITING UNTIL MORNING TO DECIDE ABOUT SPENDING TIME WITH GOD IS A RECIPE FOR FAILURE.

A strong and vibrant personal devotional life is vital if you desire to develop a Kingdom filter around your heart. Learn to appreciate the teachings of Jesus. I can't think of anything more powerful or helpful in combating the materialism of our age than the words of Jesus in the Sermon on the Mount. Paul told Timothy that the Scriptures "are able to make thee wise."[a] If there was ever a time in history when we needed God's wisdom, it would seem to be now.

Pray

Visualize once again the canal of options flowing toward you. When you were a small child, those options came slowly. Most of your decisions were made by your parents. But as you get older, you have to make more and more choices. When you finally begin bringing home that weekly paycheck, the stream of options accelerates rapidly. Now you are in control of your own money, and there seems to be an endless flow of choices. We have talked about the importance of developing a Biblical filter to help sort through all these choices, but what about all the options coming at you that the Bible does not specifically address?

Prayer will be invaluable to you. Learn to go first to the Lord when faced with difficult options. Many financial dilemmas young people get into could be avoided if they would simply begin with prayer.

I remember talking to a young man who had purchased a four-wheel-drive truck. He had not been able to pay cash for the truck, so he had started down the payment road. Several payments later, he was beginning to regret his hasty decision. "I just wish," he told me, "that I had taken some time to pray about it first and ask someone older for advice."

[a]2 Timothy 3:15

Praying and asking the Lord gives Him an opportunity to work in our hearts. Make it a habit to pray before making a major purchase. This practice will help you develop a healthy Kingdom filter in your life.

Ask Others

In our technological age, it is tempting to run to the computer when we have a question. Where at one time we would have gone to our fathers for advice, many now run to Google. But is that really a safe source? I am amazed how many financial struggles could be avoided if we would only ask someone older for advice. Be humble enough to ask.

Many of the options coming at you each day can be detrimental to your financial and spiritual life. In our youth we often see the advantage of an option more clearly than the danger. Asking someone who has been farther down the road can be extremely helpful.

I remember hearing about a get-rich-quick plan when I was a teenager. I was immediately excited. This really sounded good! All I needed to do was send a small amount of money, and the advertisement told how lots of money would start flowing back to me. I couldn't wait to get started. But I asked my father about it, and he provided another perspective. He informed me that if it sounded too good to be true, it probably was. He told me he wouldn't even waste a postage stamp on it, let alone send them money.

Shortly after that, I learned the whole plan was a fraud. My father had lived long enough to recognize it for what it was, and I was blessed by listening to his counsel.

Use Time and Technology Wisely

Recently my wife and I attended a social function in another area. We were sitting with a group of people in the same living room where in past years we had spent many hours discussing the Word of God. I always looked forward to being in this home, and I carried many good memories of leaving with a fresh desire to walk closer to the Lord.

But this time I was disappointed. Several of the young people and a couple of the older men had recently purchased new cell phones, and a good part of the day was spent comparing and discussing the features and capabilities of these phones. As I left that evening, it was with some sadness.

As believers, we are in a terrific battle. It is a spiritual battle for our hearts and minds, and ultimately for our souls. Satan is coming in like a flood, and I am concerned that we lack the spiritual discernment and discipline to be aware of his devices. Can we really afford to while away our time talking about the latest technology features? Do we understand the tactics of the enemy in this area? Are we underestimating his deceptive abilities?

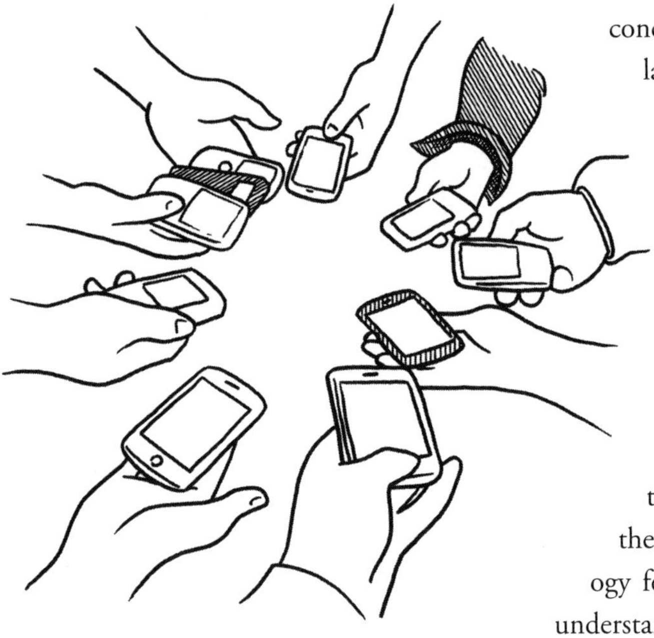

A few years ago I talked with a fellow believer who had chosen not to own a cell phone. I asked him why he had made this decision, and he explained, "I have watched many of our young people sit around all afternoon comparing phones and ring tones, and I wonder how the Lord feels about this. God has surrounded us with an amazing display of His creative power, and yet we choose to be more enamored with a phone."

This man then made an observation I have thought about many times since. "The common apple is much more amazing than any cell phone. It starts with just a few cells, pushes out by some unseen force to become a bud, and then finally, by converting sunlight and nutrients from the soil and air, becomes an apple. Why aren't we sitting around marveling at this? We should be passing an apple around the room and staring with open mouths at the amazing creativity of our God!"

Technology has the potential of robbing our awe of God Himself, and you need Spirit-inspired personal discipline to keep this from happening. Before you purchase that latest piece of technology, ask yourself a few questions. Will this item really enhance my relationship with God? Will it help me find more quiet time with God? Will I be tempted to talk of its virtues with others?

I believe we need to become much more disciplined in our choices in the area of technology if we are going to survive the onslaught of technological consumerism in our culture.

Conclusion

Survival in our materialistic culture will require personal discipline. Just as screens and filters are vital to the success of irrigation ditches, so Spirit-driven personal discipline is essential in our lives. You may belong to a family that has firm rules. You may be part of a church with established standards and guidelines. If you have these in your life, thank the Lord for them. They can be wonderful blessings if you allow them to be.

But in our age where travel is common and information readily available, I am convinced you will need more than just standards provided by others. You will need personal conviction and discipline. God has not left us without weapons against the enemy, and we need to exhort and encourage each other in the battle. Encourage others your age. Use spontaneous discussions to exhort fellow believers. And most important, let the Holy Spirit develop personal conviction and discipline in your life as protection against the enemy's attacks.

For Further Reflection

1. The man who was focused on wealth in this chapter chose not to sit down and read the newspaper. What are some steps a believer might consider to help himself stay focused on the Kingdom?

2. What are some options in life that must be filtered out because they are not compatible with a Kingdom focus? What are some choices that might be good, but not the best?

3. Share some difficulties you have had in maintaining regular devotions. What steps could you take to increase your consistency?

4. How is technology affecting your spiritual life? Are there times when it distracts you from your walk with God? Discuss ways that some personal guidelines and accountability could help.

Who Needs a Budget? | 13

TODAY THERE ARE THREE KINDS OF PEOPLE: THE HAVES, THE HAVE-NOTS, AND THE HAVE-NOT-PAID-FOR-WHAT-THEY-HAVES.

—EARL WILSON

I lived in a rural area while growing up, and I always looked forward to an opportunity to go to town. Those long aisles stocked with an amazing array of enticing items stirred something inside me. Even as a very young boy, retailing intrigued me. The thought of buying something for one price and selling it for more fascinated me. I could not imagine a simpler way to make money. It sure looked a lot easier than hoeing around our orchard trees in the hot California sun. As I worked, I watched hundreds of cars pass our driveway. I began to imagine them as potential customers, and I began to dream big dreams. I could picture a large store at the end of the lane (I would be the owner, of course) with lines of people eagerly waiting to purchase my merchandise.

I was eight years old when I decided I had thought about this long enough. Dragging an assortment of scrap lumber out from behind the barn to the middle of our circle driveway, I commenced to build. I knew every successful businessman had his own office, so it seemed clear that an office was the thing to start building. I could picture myself sitting at my desk, very involved with the business (primarily counting money) of the great enterprise I would soon be running.

What Happened to Our Driveway?

I clearly remember my father coming home that night. He was somewhat alarmed and immediately inquired about the small structure rising out of the scattered lumber in the middle of the drive. I informed him that I was building an office for my new business. I remember my father patiently suggesting that I should start with the store first and see how that went. "If the store does well," he suggested, "the office could be built later."

Of course, there were no "ifs" in my mind, but after some discussion we agreed on this plan. A few evenings later, primarily due to his carpentry skills, a small fruit stand was built. The little business really did quite well, probably due more to charitable neighbors than to the abilities of the aspiring entrepreneur. But not so well that an office was ever required. A small cash box was all I needed, and the office idea was soon forgotten.

I am thankful that my father did not just laugh off my idea. I'm sure it was tempting. To come home to an eight-year-old busily constructing a new office in the middle of the driveway is enough to test any parent's patience, and this was not the first time my father had faced a wild idea. I had plenty of enthusiasm, energy, and vision, but a shortage of direction and focus. He gave me some wise counsel and helped me properly focus my energy.

Focusing Our Finances

This is the purpose of a budget. Often youth have a strong desire to do great things for the Kingdom. They can see the goals they would like to achieve, but they have difficulty focusing all their energy and idealism to produce meaningful results. I have talked to many young people and listened to their goals. They generally admit they need some structure in their financial lives. They would like to direct more of their resources to the poor and focus more of their lives on Kingdom-building efforts, but they lack a plan to actually make it all work. Somehow the money disappears before they reach their goal.

Little Decisions

As you begin to make more of your own decisions and deal with life's many options, it is important to understand the impact of little decisions. Some financial decisions seem insignificant at the time, but if you continue to make those choices, they will greatly affect whether or not you arrive at your goal.

Let me illustrate it like this. Let's say you enjoy stopping in at the local Starbucks once in a while for coffee and a pastry. And let's also assume that this little excursion costs you $5.82 each time you do it. If you do this once a month, this habit will cost you $69.84 a year. That doesn't sound too bad. But if you decide to do this every Saturday morning, your cost each year will be $302.64. Now it looks different. You could do a lot with $300. But imagine what happens if you stop in at Starbucks every day on the way to work. Now your yearly expense is $1,513.20! Frequency of spending is as important as the amount, and without some type of budget in place, it is easy to drift.

> "FREQUENCY OF SPENDING IS AS IMPORTANT AS THE AMOUNT."

I recently visited an orphanage in El Salvador. As the administrator of the facility showed me around, I noticed he would stop briefly, tighten a dripping spigot, and then continue with the tour. I asked him later about their water situation, and he explained that their pump barely produced enough water for their needs, but they had found that by watching their water use closely, they could make do. It is surprising how much water can be wasted every day by just one dripping faucet, and if you add all the potential leaks in an orphanage, the overall effect on the water supply can be astounding.

Just a Little Here and There

Use of money in our youth can be similar to the orphanage's water problem. Many young people become convicted and would like to sponsor a child, save for a house in the future, or contribute toward literature in a persecuted country. But too often, due to a lack of planning, there are too many "drips" in their finances. A little money goes here because this was on sale, and a small amount goes there because that looked good at the time, and they suddenly realize nothing is left for things that really matter.

It is important to decide first what really matters. Spend time before the Lord asking for His guidance in deciding this. I would also encourage you to write down a vision for your life and finances. Determine what is important to you and where you really want your finances to go. You might include goals such as saving toward the purchase of a tool, a vehicle, or a home several years from now. Your vision might include Kingdom investments such as helping a particular mission or assisting an organization that focuses on feeding and clothing the poor. Go ahead and put these goals on paper.

Setting Up a Budget

Once you have established a clear vision and a direction you believe the Lord wants you to take, it is time to move forward with setting up a budget. There are many good budgets out there, and it does not need to be complicated or operated by a computer. If you have access to a computer, some good programs are available, but never purchase a computer for this purpose. Most young people do not use budgets simply because the entire process looks daunting and their expenses are minimal. However, if you can find a budgeting system that works for you and take the time to put it into practice, you will be amazed at how it can bless your life. It will train you to think differently about purchases, and this way of thinking about finances will be of value to you your entire life.

To begin organizing your finances, start tracking your expenses. Write down everything you spend, from the McDonald's coffee you bought Monday morning to your vehicle expenses. Do this for an extended period of time. Start with a month, then a year. This will help you see where your money is going, and you can make wise choices accordingly.

Setting up a budget should be easy from there. Simply determine how much you want to spend in each category.

To visualize how a budget works, let me give a very basic illustration.

Imagine that you have several coffee cans on your bedroom dresser. One is labeled "Saving," another "Giving," and others are "Clothes," "Vehicle," "Eating Out," "Miscellaneous," etc. In other words, there is a can for each area of your life that consumes part of your paycheck.

Now imagine that each time you receive a check you place a percentage of that check in each of the cans. If your paycheck was $100, for example, then you might put $25 in the savings can, $20 in the vehicle can, and so on until all of your $100 paycheck is distributed. Then as you need money during the week for eating out, for example, you would take money out of the can labeled "Eating Out." If you need money for gas, you would take money from the can labeled "Vehicle."

The beauty of this system is that it helps you know when you are spending too much in an area. If you want to purchase a new coat, you simply look in the "Clothes" coffee can and see if you have enough money to purchase the coat. This simple method can help you know what you can afford and can help you stay focused on reaching goals, such as saving or giving, that really matter to you. It should be remembered, however, that just because there is money in the can does not mean it needs to be spent. Our goal should be to move as many of our resources as possible toward the Kingdom.

JUST BECAUSE THERE IS MONEY IN THE CAN DOES NOT MEAN IT NEEDS TO BE SPENT.

While this method is simple, most of us do not want coffee cans full of cash on our dressers. But you can do the same thing on paper. Find a system that works for you. If you don't want to devise your own system, the *Budgeting Made Simple*[1] workbook has forms and charts set up to help with budgeting and other aspects of financial management.

Regardless of what system you use, it is important to learn to organize your life and finances in some way. Even if you decide that your finances do not warrant a detailed budget, I want to encourage you to take some organizational steps in your life. Some of this may seem unimportant now, but as your life becomes more complex and you are called upon to make more choices, you will be thankful you have a plan in place.

Let's look at a few ways you can achieve your vision of using your finances to bless the Kingdom.

Immediate Deposit

During the last ten years a concept called "pay yourself first" has become very popular. The idea is to immediately take a certain percentage out of every paycheck and deposit it into a savings account. Then use the balance of your income for normal day-to-day expenses. This has caught on because people tend to spend whatever is in their checkbooks. If you don't put your savings in your checking account, you don't spend your savings.

Even our government understands this concept. If you notice, they do not wait to take their taxes from a paycheck until after they see how an employee's month goes. No, they take taxes out of your check before you ever see it. This ensures they actually receive the money. You can do the same, and I would highly recommend this. It can be accomplished in different ways. Some have it set up so the bank automatically deposits a certain amount in savings each month. Others do this when taking their check into the bank. If your payroll check is for $500 and you have decided to deposit 10 percent each month into a special account, then you would deposit $50 into your special account and $450 into your regular checking account. This ensures that 10 percent of your income always goes into this account, even if you overspend and empty your checking account.

Next let's look at things you should consider having special accounts for.

Invest in the Kingdom First

If you take the time to write out a vision for your life, you will find some priorities there. And if you have a desire to live for the Kingdom of Jesus, one of your top priorities will be to invest money where Jesus would want it invested. There will be very few times in your life when it will be easy to give. It seems there are always more things we want than money available to buy them. But you will also find it easier to save while you are young than at almost any other time. If you are living at home and your parents are paying most of your living expenses, it is an excellent time to learn to give.

Spend time considering Kingdom options. Read newsletters, talk to others who have experience helping those in need, and then start investing. Many young people can give more than 10 percent of their income during this time, and you should hold this up before the Lord. But make sure at least a portion of your giving is done regularly. Make investing in the Kingdom a primary reason for going to work each day. You will find this will change your perspective and your attitude regarding your job.

Save for the Future

It is also important to consider saving while you are young. As we saw earlier, people typically have more discretionary income available during this time of life. You know some expenses are coming. Vehicles, homes, and even tools for your occupation are all good reasons to set some money aside. Do not wait till the expense is upon you to begin planning for it. This is how many people fall into the endless cycle of debt.

But it is also important to make saving second priority. You don't know whether you will actually live long enough to need that vehicle, live in that home, or use those tools. But you do know of needs right now that some of "your" money should be going toward. Ask the Lord to help you as you allocate your income. I would encourage you to even have separate accounts for savings and giving. These categories should be primary at this point in your life, so make sure money is allocated for giving and saving before beginning to spend that paycheck.

Create a Basic Filing System

Another thing to consider and implement in your life is a basic filing system. I say "basic" because it does not need to be anything elaborate. You can purchase a very small file box that will work nicely. Have file folders for your bank statements, your vehicle expenses, and receipts for major purchases. Avoid having a pile of papers on your dresser. You will find that a little organization will make your life much more efficient.

If you have a particular area of interest, have a file where anything pertaining to that topic can be saved. If you are giving to a certain organization, keep all the information regarding that endeavor in a file. Then when you have questions or need to find a particular receipt, you know where to go. Just a little effort in this area can help develop a pattern that will bless you in the future.

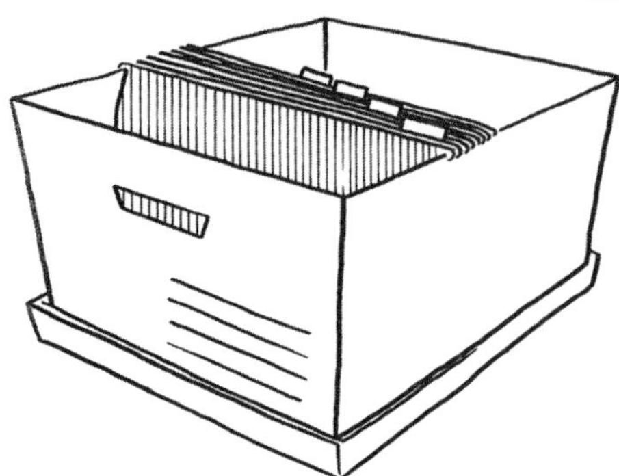

Keep Bills Paid

Setting up a basic filing system will also help you keep your bills paid. There are few things that damage a believer's witness to the world more than a reputation for late or unpaid bills. If you cannot pay a bill on time, pick up the phone and call. Keeping your finances up to date, even if the payment is going to your parents, is a sign of spiritual maturity. Failure to be prompt can bring reproach on the name of Jesus in your neighborhood.

Late payments can also damage your credit score and hinder your opportunity for borrowing in the future. Being late just once can lower your credit score by as much as 10 percent and can stay on your record for up to seven years. This credit score is sometimes used to determine the percentage rate you are given when applying for a home mortgage, so just a little carelessness can be costly for many years.

Conclusion

It is easy to neglect organization in your youth. There are so many exciting things to be involved in and activities to participate in. Who wants to waste time sitting around worrying about budgets, organizing filing systems, and opening savings accounts? I understand; I was young myself. But as we conclude this chapter, I would like you to consider two things.

First, keep in mind that the future comes very quickly. Just as it seems it wasn't very long ago that you were in grade school, so it will not be long until you are looking back at these teenage years wondering how they went so fast. My hope is that you will not look back with regret.

Second, remember you are establishing life patterns now that will be hard to change later. It is much easier to develop a love for the Kingdom and a proper focus for your finances now than it will be when the pressures and cares of life begin to press upon you. May the Lord bless you as you consider this area of budgeting and financial organization.

For Further Reflection

1. This chapter talked about "little drips" in our finances. Identify some of those drips, or seemingly insignificant expenses, that add up over time.

2. Have you made an attempt to budget in the past? If so, share your experience and what you learned from it.

3. Discuss the advantage of the "pay yourself first" system. How could you implement this in your life?

4. Discuss some potential percentages that could be used in budgeting. What percentage should a young man save? How much could he give for the Kingdom?

Choosing a Career | 14

A MAN WHO ROLLS UP HIS SHIRT SLEEVES IS RARELY IN DANGER OF LOSING HIS SHIRT.

—**ANONYMOUS**

"So, what do you want to do for a living when you grow up?"

We are asked this question many times in our younger years. In fact, most of us learn to dread it. Well-meaning adults ask, trying to determine how far we are looking down the road, and perhaps even encouraging us to seriously consider our future. But most of us would rather avoid the question because we are not sure. Many of us, and especially young men, go through phases in life when our interests vary. We want to be firemen or operate the huge loaders and excavators we see along the road. We have a longing, even in our youth, to be significant. We want jobs that accomplish something momentous and make us feel needed.

I remember working with my father on a construction site during my teenage years. The customer came out to observe our progress, and as he was standing there he asked, "So, Gary, what kind of work would you like to do for the rest of your life?"

I did not know what to say. My father had always been a carpenter, and whenever I went to work with him, I ended up with the task of cleaning up. So I told him I didn't know what I was going to do, but I did know what I was *not* going to do for a living. I sure wasn't going to work in construction. I have been teased about this response for years, since I spent the next twenty-five years doing nothing but construction.

So, What Are You Going to Do?

One of the reasons this question is difficult is because we have so many options. It hasn't always been this way. In the past most people

gave little thought to their future occupations. Their lives were centered on survival. They knew they needed work to purchase food and pay the bills, and jobs were not easy to find. But in our time the options are almost endless. There are even businesses to help you find the job that fits your personality and abilities. Occupations have become extremely specialized, and a person can find careers that specialize in almost anything. Sometimes the array of options can seem daunting.

It can be like standing at an intersection where many roads come together. Coming expenses tell us one of these roads must be chosen, but how can we know which is best? We look off into the distance, trying to see where each road leads. We want the path that will work out best. But there are hills, curves, and obstructions, and it is difficult to see very far. We ask others for advice, and often their opinions differ. So, which path is best? How can you make a decision today regarding your occupation that you will not regret tomorrow?

It would be nice if I could simply offer you a pair of career binoculars—some way you could look down each of these roads and clearly see the future. However, only God knows the future of our economy and the outlook for the many occupational options out there today. But I would like to offer a few words of advice in your search. God has not left us alone in any part of our lives, and He has given us tools we can use in making major decisions like this. But before we look at some of these tools, it is important to give some thought to the amazing changes taking place in our world.

Sweeping Change

A revolution is taking place in our world economy and job market that will have repercussions around the globe for years to come.

Our world is getting smaller. A string of technological inventions has transformed how we communicate and do business. First came the telegraph and telephone. For the first time, men could communicate without sharing the same space. Then came the computer and the ability to compute and store vast quantities of information. But it was really the combination of these two inventions, the telephone and the computer, that empowered both inventions and changed forever the way business is transacted. Today people around the world can exchange and move vast quantities of information almost instantly.

So, how does this affect occupations today? There is no way to project all the ways the Internet has changed and will continue to change occupations. In 2005 Thomas Friedman, an internationally known author and journalist, wrote a book called *The World Is Flat.*[1] This bestseller was his attempt to wake up America. As a nation we have become lazy, he warned. Our work ethic has deteriorated and our populace is primarily interested in ease of lifestyle. In the past, America could protect good wages for her citizens simply through immigration laws. Now, Friedman's book says, a major change has taken place. By using the Internet, people from Bangladesh can compete directly with workers in New York. This has a huge effect on jobs in many occupations.

For example, look for a moment at the accounting industry. For years many of us went to our local accountant for our tax work. He took our information, filled out the proper tax forms, and gave us the forms to sign and mail in. But change came to the industry. In 2003 approximately 25,000 U.S. tax returns were done in India. In 2004 that number rose to 100,000, and by 2005 it was about 400,000.[2] This type of outsourcing is invading many industries, and the attraction is obvious. While an accountant in America might expect to make $60,000 to $80,000 a year or even more, an accountant in India might be very happy to earn $5,000 a year.

These changes are not just happening in high-paying professional jobs. There are experimental programs in which the voice you hear at the fast food drive-thru is actually someone taking your order from another country. After all, why pay someone $10 an hour plus holidays and vacation time to take orders when there are many qualified workers in foreign countries who would be glad to earn $10 a day?

All of these changes will have repercussions on our occupations in the future. If your daily work can be transferred by the Internet, you should take warning. But even if your business is not directly affected, you should take note. In many of our trades, we work for some of the professionals whose jobs are being transferred. As these jobs are eliminated, everyone will be affected. America has enjoyed a long season of prosperity while much of the world has suffered. We have lived high on the global hill, but if Thomas Friedman is correct, those days may be over. The world is becoming flat.

I don't believe our Lord would want us to be overly concerned about these changes. He is still in control and still cares for His people. And the changes will also create new jobs. But I believe young men should value their jobs more now than they have in the past. There is still work for the willing man in America. That isn't true in every country, and it may not always be the situation here.

I worked with a man several years ago who had no loyalty to his employer and felt free to let that be known. "I will go across the street," he would proclaim, "if the man over there will pay me a nickel more an hour."

This man was a talented cabinetmaker, and due to his philosophy, he had worked for almost every cabinetmaker in town. But this kind of reputation does not portray the Kingdom of God to seekers. Paul told Titus, "Exhort servants to be obedient unto their own masters, and to please them well in all things; not answering again; not purloining, but showing all good fidelity; that they may adorn the doctrine of God our Saviour in all things."[a] Occupations are not just to obtain money. God wants us to use our occupations to expand and strengthen the Kingdom of God.

Choosing an Occupation

So what does all this change mean for us, and how are we to know which path to take? As you stand at the intersection where these occu-

[a]Titus 2:9-10

pational roads meet and try to discern the best path for yourself, how are you to know? Choosing a career is a major decision that will affect your whole life, including your ministry to others. Let's look at a few steps you can take that will help you make a proper decision.

It is of utmost importance to spend time in prayer over this decision. Regardless of how many facts you have and how sure you are, spend time in prayer. God may have much greater things in mind than you ever imagined. There are curves and detours in the road ahead that only God knows and understands. Be sure to ask Him as you proceed. Do not hesitate to ask your parents to pray with you. You will find the prayers of others to be a great blessing.

Are You Using a Cash or Kingdom Perspective?

Recently I saw a newspaper article regarding occupations and income. The bold title proclaimed: "See what your neighbor is earning!" This article contained page after page of people from almost every occupation imaginable. Just below each picture was the person's name and yearly income. I picked up the paper and scanned the occupations. A firefighter who earned $45,000 was next to a country singer who had been paid $18,000,000 during the same year. A teacher's aide who brought home $15,400 was next to golf champion Tiger Woods, whose income added up to over $110,000,000. Row after row of all types of individuals were accompanied by their yearly incomes.

> A PERSON'S SALARY IS LIKE A SCORE IN OUR CULTURE. THE HIGHER YOUR SCORE, THE MORE SIGNIFICANT YOU ARE.

Americans like this kind of thing. We are interested in a person's salary. It is like a score in our culture. The higher your score, the more significant you are.

It is important, as we look at tools that can help determine which occupational path to take, to avoid using society's scorecard. While income is important and can even be used for Kingdom work, other features of an occupation are much more important. As you consider and analyze occupations, learn to do it from a Kingdom perspective.

Examine Careers From a Kingdom Perspective

Will this occupation have Kingdom-building opportunities? In other words, will you be able to achieve more than just bringing home a check? I'm not saying that providing an income for our families is not important. But I am saying we should be open to opportunities to do more. Some careers have inherent potential for reaching out to the lost or encouraging those who are discouraged. Imagine the potential ministry, for example, in being the maintenance man at a nursing home or hospital. I know people who have changed careers, not because of increased income, but simply because of potential ministry. I know of many who could be earning much more but have chosen their occupations because they allow them to further the Kingdom while still earning an income.

If marriage is a possibility in your future, then some consideration should be taken as to how each potential occupation could affect your home. Will you be able to be home in the evenings? Many jobs require travel and time away from home. This should be considered. It is extremely important to be home as much as possible while raising a family.

Another feature to consider is whether or not your occupation would allow your children to participate. Could small children work with you during their formative years? For many years I worked in commercial construction. The laws were strict, and taking small children along was forbidden. But working can be helpful in young children's development. They need to feel needed, and few things can fulfill that need like physical labor.

Identify Your Assets

When choosing an occupation, it is important to identify your assets. What are your physical and mental abilities? What kinds of opportunities and options do you have? Is there a family business available? The Lord has given each of us different abilities. Some thrive on figuring out solutions to dilemmas mentally, and they enjoy sitting at a desk all day. Others feel a need to be outside and active. There is a place for both, but it is important to give some thought to this. God has made each of us different. Accept yourself the way God made you, and don't spend time wishing your options or abilities were different.

Sometimes, in our preoccupation with wishing things were different, we ignore great potential at our fingertips. When we think of successes during the gold rush, we tend to visualize men who found large veins of gold and were able to extract great wealth from their mines. But the truth is, those men were very few. Many of the men who did well sold picks, shovels, and supplies to those in search of easy money. These merchants had a more realistic view of the opportunity at the time.

THE MERCHANTS WHO SOLD SUPPLIES TO THOSE IN SEARCH OF EASY MONEY HAD A MORE REALISTIC VIEW OF THE OPPORTUNITY AT THE TIME.

The Lord has placed each person in a unique setting and with different talents. It is tempting, if you are involved in farming or a certain trade, to conclude that everyone else should be as well—that since this occupation is a blessing to your family, this occupation is best for others as well. But God has made each one as it has pleased Him, and it is important to look at our assets as gifts from Him. In the Bible we read of God giving special gifts to certain men. Bezaleel was given special ability to work with his hands on the tabernacle, and I believe God still equips men and women today for special jobs.[b]

Understand, too, that many jobs can be used for the Kingdom. I have worked with young men who had a gift for reaching out to the hurting on the jobsite. One man in particular comes to mind. He was a diligent worker and always tried to do his best, and his natural friendliness and openness made others open up to him. I saw him repeatedly reach out to others in the middle of a busy work day and inquire about their spiritual lives. He always did it in a quiet way that put people at

[b]Exodus 36:1

ease. But he was able to show concern for others without being distracted and without distracting others from the work at hand. He was not just working for the contractor; he was working for the King!

What Are You Hearing From Those Who Are Older?

Imagine arriving in California during the gold rush. You have left everything in the East to go west in pursuit of wealth. After a long, difficult, dangerous journey, you finally crest the last hill and come down into the Sacramento Valley. After finding a place to camp, you take care of your livestock and head into town. Now remember, you have come here looking for gold, but the area is unfamiliar. All you know is there is treasure in California, you are running out of supplies, and if you are going to continue eating, you need to find some gold.

What is the first thing you would do? I suspect the first thing most prospectors did was ask the people in town where gold was being found. These folks in town had been there longer, and they probably knew where miners were experiencing success. They also knew where people had failed and could tell stories of prospectors gone bust. You would want to listen to all of this before deciding where to dig. Asking people who have been there longer and had more experience could save you a lot of wasted time and effort.

This same principle applies when deciding on a career. One of the best resources you have is the older people around you. They have been here longer. They have watched as others have tried certain paths. They have seen both successes and failures.

Most of us have parents, leaders in the church, and older individuals in our church communities whose lives have exhibited a love for the Kingdom of God. You can go to them with confidence that, although their advice may not always be perfect, they will at least try to encourage you toward a safe path.

Conclusion

Your occupation will have a great impact on your entire life and ministry, and for some it can be a difficult decision. But I want to encourage you, wherever you are. You may be in a family farming operation or a family construction business. You may feel guilty and fear that you have not given the Kingdom enough thought in deciding on an occupation. If God calls you to walk away from a family business that was handed to you, then do it. Some of the apostles had to leave their family businesses to be used by the Lord.

On the other hand, do not assume that since you didn't give much thought to your occupation, God cannot use you there. I firmly believe God calls different people to different places, and He is able to use them there. Some have had to leave their businesses. Moses and Elisha were both called to leave occupations they had become comfortable with, yet Paul kept on making tents while he preached the Gospel. Our primary focus should be that all is done to the glory of God. Whether you find yourself out on a tractor or working in a public setting, may you have a Kingdom-driven desire that the Lord Jesus be magnified through your occupation.

For Further Reflection

1. What are some occupations that might be a hindrance to spiritual and family life?

2. Make a list of occupations that could bless a community as well as provide opportunities to reach out to others.

3. Discuss some of the changes that are occurring in the job market. What are some occupations that could be moved overseas in the future? How much thought should we give to this when choosing an occupation?

4. If a man has a family, what kinds of jobs would allow him to work with his children? What types would make it difficult for them to participate in?

Money and Marriage | 15

NEVER MARRY FOR MONEY. YE'LL BORROW IT CHEAPER.

—SCOTTISH PROVERB

I sat in the high school cafeteria and listened as Jane told me her dilemma. Ronald had been courting her for many months, and everything seemed to be going fine. But now Jane wasn't sure. She told of several events that had caused her to stop and wonder how responsible Ronald really was. But each time uncertainty had filled her heart, Jane had talked to Ronald, and he had explained everything.

"Now," said Jane with anguish in her voice, "he just went out and blew $700 on a new rifle he doesn't need. I can't believe he did that. He already owes several people money, but it seems every time he gets a little money in his pocket, he just can't wait to spend it!"

These doubts continued to bother Jane, and it was not long until Ronald and Jane's courtship terminated. I was friends with Ronald as well, and he never could understand what the big deal was. Why make such a big issue over how a man spends a little money? But I have watched Ronald and Jane over the years. Jane went on to marry a responsible Christian man, and they have a godly family. Ronald's life has been much different. His irresponsible tendencies have affected every part of his life. His financial, marital, and spiritual life is in shambles. While he can probably explain why it is all someone else's fault, the results are too obvious to ignore. Jane was absolutely right in refusing to marry a young man who could not handle his money.

In this chapter we want to look at money and marriage, and especially how a young person's ability to deal with it should be regarded. If you are courting someone, how much thought should be given to how he or she handles money? Does it matter whether he or she is part of a wealthy family or a poor one? What about your special friend's views on saving money, debt, or how nice of a home one should have? Should you worry about any of this? Should you even talk about money before you are married?

I believe some basic Biblical principles can help answer these questions.

Why Does Money Matter?

Many couples neglect talking about money, either because they do not see the point in addressing the topic, or because they end up arguing when they try. But why did Jesus spend so much time talking about money? Why didn't He just leave the natural, mundane things of life alone and focus on the spiritual? Jesus answered that question by saying, "For where your treasure is, there will your heart be also."[a] Find out what a man values, and you will have found the location of his heart.

> FIND OUT WHAT A MAN VALUES, AND YOU WILL HAVE FOUND THE LOCATION OF HIS HEART.

Observing how your potential spouse uses money will tell you a lot about his or her heart. If vast quantities of his money tend to end up in the sporting goods store, you are learning about his heart and focus in life. If her money keeps flowing into the shoe store long after she has plenty to wear, again, you are learning about her heart. If you are in a courtship relationship, you should be comfortable talking about the use of money. If your friend is not willing to be challenged in these areas, you are again learning about his or her heart and direction in life. All of us are at different stages of growth in these areas, and we need to have charity with each other. But we also should be able to discuss our use of money and be open to accountability.

Does It Matter if His Parents Are Wealthy?

Does it matter how much money your prospective in-laws have? Marriage without regard to financial standing is a relatively new idea.

[a]Matthew 6:21

For centuries marriages were arranged by parents and were often based completely on social status and wealth. In our day, however, wealth is often not even considered. Those entering into marriage might come from completely different financial backgrounds. This can create conflict in a new home.

Perhaps one marriage partner grew up being very frugal and based decisions almost solely on cost, and the other might tend to make decisions on the basis of convenience. One may be accustomed to eating in restaurants and makes selections based on what sounds good to eat. The other looks down the right-hand side of the menu first and makes choices almost exclusively on price. In these situations there can be conflict if there is no communication.

Different backgrounds can bring many challenges. If a wife has grown up in an affluent setting, for example, and her husband is not able to support the lifestyle she regards as normal, this can strain the relationship. But different backgrounds do not need to stress a marriage unduly. I can think of marriages where one was raised surrounded by everything wealth could afford, and the other in the midst of frugality. But as couples they have committed themselves to Kingdom living and are shining examples of a simple lifestyle. There is very little that can stand in the way if a young couple is committed to living for the Kingdom and willing to communicate.

What About Debt, Savings, and Retirement?

Our view of life is shaped by the homes we grow up in. Some families use debt frequently. It becomes a way of life to borrow when things are a little tight. In other homes, consumer debt is not even an option.

When money is tight, they spend less and do without. Some families always have plenty of everything, and money is rarely discussed. In others, money is scarce and is a daily topic of conversation. All of this affects young children and will quite naturally shape their financial views.

It is important to discuss these differences during courtship. Don't start with the premise that your home was right; rather, be open about your differences while searching for a safe path with a Kingdom perspective for the two of you. These discussions will reveal much about your potential spouse's financial views, and more than that, will reveal the strength of his or her love for the Kingdom. Very few discussions will tell you more about a believer's commitment to the Kingdom than a heart-to-heart talk about finances.

"VERY FEW DISCUSSIONS WILL TELL YOU MORE ABOUT A BELIEVER'S COMMITMENT TO THE KINGDOM THAN A HEART-TO-HEART TALK ABOUT FINANCES."

Share your views on debt. Do you feel you should borrow money? Do you feel differently about different types of debt? Talk about savings. Do you think it is right to save for known expenses like car replacement? What about all the unknowns in life? Should believers save for events that might happen to them—things like medical catastrophes and natural disasters?

What about retirement? Discuss how you view retirement and planning for it. Should Christians ever voluntarily retire? Should they save toward that time of life? Can you find anything in the Bible regarding retirement? Should children take care of their parents during those years? Talk about how this could work and how it could affect your finances. All of these questions are real issues, and there is no better time to begin talking than during courtship. Young people who have a passion to live for the Kingdom should never run out of discussion topics. Any young couple who desires to build a home on Scriptural principles should spend time discussing how the teachings of Jesus can be lived out practically in their lives.

Renting Versus Owning a Home

There has been much discussion in the past few years about the advantages of owning your home versus renting one. Historically, housing has been a good investment. While we do not know the future, we can assume, if history repeats itself, that housing will continue to be a good long-term investment. For years the prevailing wisdom said it was always better to own. In those inflationary years when homes continued to escalate in value, money spent on rent was viewed as foolishness, as just throwing your money away. But times have changed, and suddenly the question is not quite as simple as it once was.

Homes in many areas have seen a major loss in value, and conventional wisdom doesn't seem quite as wise. Young families who saved for that initial down payment have watched the value of the home they purchased drop until they owe more on the house than it is worth. In many of these situations they would have been ahead financially if they had rented. We don't know if homes will continue to lose value or if they will rebound, but we have learned that homes can lose substantial value in a short time.

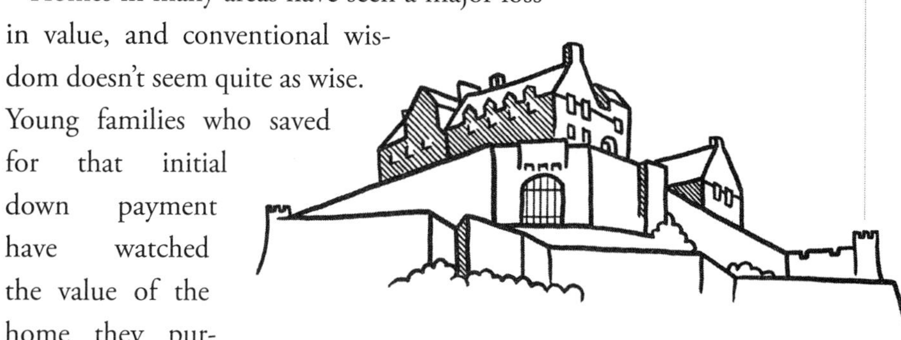

The other issue is whether owning a home actually costs more, due to our inclination toward home improvement. When a couple rents a home, they tend to view it as shelter. They pay the rent, live in it, and understand that it is not theirs—that sometime they will turn it back over to the landlord. There is typically very little pride in a rented home.

But when we own a home, we are inclined to spend more on interior decorations and improvements. It can become much more than just protection against the elements. Homes in our culture have become an expression of who we are and how much we are worth.

Some families forgo this temptation by renting and attempting to focus their time and money on the Kingdom. They understand the disadvantages to renting and that it is possible to save money in the long term by owning, but they choose to rent to avoid the continual home-improvement temptation.

There may not be a right or wrong answer to this question, but I believe it is important to discuss it before marriage. The prophet many years ago asked, "Can two walk together, except they be agreed?"[b] This is still a valid question. Courtship is the time to discuss the overriding vision for your lives. Ensure that your potential spouse has a vision for building the Kingdom of Jesus Christ, and make sure you can unite your visions. Take the opportunity to make sure your partner is serious enough about Kingdom living that he or she is willing to sacrifice for that vision.

Conclusion

In my teenage years, I got to know a young man who was courting a young lady. I knew both of them very well, and I had some concerns about their relationship. There were some major differences in their vision and direction, so one evening I asked my friend if they ever discussed their differences when they spent time together. I still remember being shocked by his reply. "No," he said. "We have tried talking about that several times, and every time we get into an argument. After a few arguments we just decided not to discuss it anymore. We seem to get along better if we leave it alone."

> "YOU MAY BE ABLE TO AVOID SOME ISSUES DURING COURTSHIP, EVEN BIG ISSUES. BUT YOU WILL NOT BE ABLE TO AVOID THEM AFTER YOU ARE MARRIED."

Their goal seemed to be to have a nice evening and avoid conflict at all costs. This couple eventually married, and sadly, to this day they

[b]Amos 3:3

live in conflict.

You may be able to avoid some issues during courtship, even big issues. But you will not be able to avoid them after you are married. It is important to discuss financial matters honestly and openly early in a relationship. Spend time seeking the Lord's will in your lives when you are together. Take time to open His Word together and examine Jesus' teaching on money and possessions. When a young man and woman can unite on vision, devoting their lives and finances to the Lord, they can become a powerful force for the Kingdom.

For Further Reflection

1. As a young woman considers marrying a young man, what would be some warning signs she could watch for as he uses his finances? In what ways could his use of money demonstrate a Kingdom focus?

2. List some financial issues and viewpoints that should be discussed before marriage.

3. Discuss the advantages and disadvantages of owning versus renting a home.

4. What chapters in the Bible could a young couple study as they develop a Kingdom-focused view of their finances?

Single Life—Serving Without Distraction | 16

HE THAT IS UNMARRIED CARETH FOR THE THINGS THAT BELONG TO THE LORD, HOW HE MAY PLEASE THE LORD.
1 CORINTHIANS 7:32

"Do you know of something I could be involved in that could be a blessing to someone?"

This question came from a single lady who called me one day. She went on to explain that she had a good job with good pay and several weeks of paid vacation every year. She had no debt, plenty of money at her disposal, and thirteen weeks of unused paid vacation she could use at any time. Her vacation time was unused simply because she did not know what to do with it. But God had been working in her heart, and she really wanted to bless the Kingdom in some way.

This lady went on to explain her feelings. "I have been on trips with other singles to Europe several times and made trips to the Holy Lands, but all of this seems empty after a while. Isn't there a way I could use my time and money to be a blessing to someone?"

I knew enough about this lady to know she had not been sitting around doing nothing. She had been actively assisting others in her local area, and yet she felt God calling her to more. She was verbalizing a question that burns in the hearts of many singles. With all the focus on the purpose and beauty of the godly family and raising children, what are singles supposed to do? What does God have in mind for those of us who do not have a spouse or children?

A Blessing to the Kingdom

Before we address these questions, I would like to share a few observations I have made regarding singles and their place in the Kingdom. First, as I think of the blessing singles are to the body of Christ, certain faces come to mind—individuals who are actively serving the Lord and have no idea how much they are accomplishing. They are using the resources God has given them and are active builders within the Kingdom. In fact, when I think of believers who are passionate about living for the Kingdom, some of the first faces I see are singles. God uses them in His Kingdom in powerful ways.

Second, I also believe singles are often ignored and unsupported. When a young mother asks for advice on how to train her children or needs someone to take care of them while she is going through a difficult time, we know what to do. But when a single feels unfulfilled and feels the Lord's calling to do more than just make money and mow the lawn, we don't always know how to respond.

I want to encourage those of you who have chosen to live single lives for the sake of the Kingdom. I know this may not be the case for all of you who are unmarried, and yet I know of some who could have married and have chosen not to. They, as the Apostle Paul said, have chosen to live single that they "may attend upon the Lord without distraction."[a]

She Never Knew

I remember a time many years ago when my wife was overwhelmed as a young mother. She'd had some difficult medical issues and now, due to a church event in our area, we had many visitors coming to stay for several days. With little ones to take care of and things around the house having been neglected due to her sickness, life seemed overwhelming. But I remember my wife receiving a phone call from a single woman who lived in another state. We hardly knew her, but she called asking if she could come a few days before the event and help out.

I came home from work to find this woman washing our windows and doing small tasks around the house. I am sure we thanked her profusely, but there was really no way for her to understand how much she had accomplished. Her gift of time changed my wife's outlook on life, demonstrated to my children what Kingdom living looks like, and encouraged me to devote my life more completely to God. That single lady has no idea how many times over the many years since

[a] 1 Corinthians 7:35

then I have thought about her selfless gift of time.

A Special Role in the Kingdom

Single life is not something to be feared. Rather, it should be embraced and used for the Kingdom. There are places to fill in the body that can be filled only by singles. I was reminded of this recently while spending the night at a mission in Haiti. I have had the opportunity to stop in at many missions, and I have gained a tremendous appreciation for the singles who work there. It is not a glorious place to be. I've listened to them in the evenings telling of their loneliness, wishing they could be home for Christmas, or longing to see new nieces and nephews.

But I have also watched them the next morning as they began their day. Many of them work in medical clinics and daily tackle problems that would tax our world's best physicians. I have watched extremely poor patients with major problems approach these missionaries with their needs, and the expressions on their poverty-stricken faces tell it all. These hurting people are not seeing an insecure young man or woman—they are seeing the face of Jesus Himself. They are feeling His touch and hearing His voice. As I have watched, I have pondered: Who else could be doing this? There is no way a young mother could dedicate the time needed to really care for all these hurting people the way these singles do.

> THESE HURTING PEOPLE ARE NOT SEEING AN INSECURE YOUNG MAN OR WOMAN—THEY ARE SEEING THE FACE OF JESUS HIMSELF.

Advantages of Singlehood

As you consider the life before you, I want you to consider some of the blessings inherent to being single. Most of us who are older and married have times of wanting to be more involved in some Kingdom-building project, but we are hindered by one of two things: time or money. Maybe we hear of a need for help somewhere after a hurricane. We would love to go, but we can't get off work, or perhaps we cannot afford the trip. Or we have an elderly neighbor who could really use someone to stop in and help on a regular basis. We would love to help out, but it seems we never get our own list of home maintenance tasks completed, and our children need our time.

An Amazing Opportunity

Singles, especially those who still live with their parents, have an amazing opportunity and advantage. Many have both time and money at their disposal. For the single who really has a passion for the Kingdom of God, the possibilities are almost endless. An incredible amount can be accomplished, and is being accomplished, by these singles.

Recently I had the opportunity to travel with an older single man who travels to devastated areas immediately following natural disasters and works behind the scenes to prepare for work teams. These work teams have a wonderful opportunity to show hurting people what Christianity really looks like. Some of these opportunities occur in countries normally hostile to Christians, so these disasters provide an open door to promote the Kingdom. But none of this would be possible if not for this man's willingness to go by himself first. It's a lonely job, and very few people even know the part he plays in the project. But as he quietly said, "This is something I can do that many can't."

Choosing to Open the Door

Think of life for a moment as a long hallway with many doors. Each door represents a choice that we face, a decision that must be made. Behind every door is a pathway that leads to even more doors. Each door represents not only a decision, but also another series of choices that must be made. Our only job then is to either open the door before us or refuse. We have little control over the doors that face us; God sets them in front of us. We only decide whether or not to walk through. Sometimes we don't like any of the doors. We scan the options, and none of them look very good. If you are young, single, and not currently involved in a relationship with a prospective spouse, it is easy to just sit down and wait until God decides to change the scenery.

Maybe none of the doors look very appealing. Perhaps you already have in mind the door you want to walk through. Maybe you have stared at the virtual door of marriage and children so long that it has become a mirage in your mind.

Serving While You Are Single

I want to encourage you to shift your eyes over to a door that God has before you right now. That is the doorway of serving while you are single. Instead of continually staring at a door that isn't even there, go ahead and walk through the one that is. Don't waste time pacing up and down the hall looking for a different door. Instead, view this time as an opportunity to actively serve the King. If you choose to walk through the door of serving while you are single, I don't know where you will end up. You may find such fulfillment that the door to marriage will be forgotten. Or maybe the door to marriage is just behind the door of serving while you're single. But regardless of what the Lord may have in mind, go ahead and walk through the door God has placed before you. You will find blessing and fulfillment that is unattainable to someone who insists on sitting in the hallway.

Conclusion

I believe God calls those who are single to use this time for the Kingdom. I also believe that God will continue to call individuals to choose a life of serving without distraction. The Bible is clear that being single is not for everyone. But it is also very clear that there are amazing blessings and opportunities available to those who will avail themselves of its benefits.

I have been blessed by watching the life of the lady who contacted me wanting to do more for the Kingdom several years ago. I have observed her as she developed a burden and a vision for Kingdom service that has inspired others. She simply took her abilities, her time, and her money and made them available to God, and He has blessed her efforts.

May the Lord bless you as you consider what God has in store for you, and may you find fulfillment as you choose to willingly and cheerfully walk through the doorway of serving while you are single.

For Further Reflection

1. In light of 1 Corinthians 7, what advantages do singles have in serving the Lord?

2. What are some activities young people can be involved in locally that can be a blessing to the local church?

3. Can you share a time when you didn't like any of the options God had before you? A time when you rejected all of the options and became ineffective in God's service?

4. Think of individuals who have been good examples of living for the Kingdom while single. Describe how their lives contributed to the Kingdom.

Investing in the Kingdom | 17

THE POOREST MAN IN THE WORLD
IS HE WHO HAS NOTHING BUT MONEY.

—JOHN D. ROCKEFELLER

We have a little one-year-old girl living with us. When she first came, she was just learning to crawl. At first all she could do was get up on her hands and knees and rock back and forth. But gradually she learned, and it was not long until she was moving rapidly across the floor. But even though crawling was great, she was not content. She watched the rest of the family standing and walking around the house, and she wanted to give it a try.

Before long we saw her stand up beside the sofa and even walk along it. But she refused to let go and step away from the furniture. Taking steps without holding on was simply outside her comfort zone. She got to where she would stand up in the middle of a room with nothing to hang on to, but she still would not take steps. This went on for a good while. There was nothing like the security of having something tangible to hold on to, and she wasn't interested in letting go. We tried various ways to entice her to take steps, but her fear was just too great.

But finally the day came when she took her first step. With arms outstretched toward an adult, she stepped away from the furniture. Once she was able to forget the sofa and take that first step, everything changed. Suddenly the world looked entirely different, and life would never be the same.

We are like that toddler circling the sofa. We want every part of our lives to bless the Lord, but commitment to regular giving is a difficult first step. We like to be in control, and letting go and committing to giving a certain percentage of our income can be difficult.

Old Testament Giving

In the Old Testament, God asked His people to give 10 percent of their income back to Him. But this was not all that God required.[a] In fact, some have estimated that if an Israelite gave all that God required, it would have added up to around 23 percent of his income.[1] It must be remembered, however, that this money was also used to operate their government, so a portion of the funds could be regarded like our income tax.

In addition to tithing, there were the gifts of first fruits, voluntary offerings, and almsgiving. It is obvious in the Old Testament that God wanted tithing to be a sort of baseline for their giving. Ten percent of their income was to be the minimum, the starting point of their giving to the Lord. God instigated the tithe, yet it seems clear He also desired voluntary sharing. Even then, God wanted hearts that responded out of thankfulness for His goodness to them.

Give Regularly

Put yourself in the place of the toddler. Why doesn't she let go of the sofa? She knows she can stand. Why not just let go? It's because of fear, isn't it? She has fallen before and does not want to experience it again.

Now consider making a commitment to regular giving. Why is this so difficult? Many young people who have no qualms about signing a two-year cell phone contract seem troubled about committing to regular giving. It's a little like letting go of the sofa. Our minds start to think of all the things that might happen. What about loss of income, unexpected expenses, or even being unable to follow an impulse

MANY YOUNG PEOPLE WHO HAVE NO QUALMS ABOUT SIGNING A TWO-YEAR CELL PHONE CONTRACT SEEM TROUBLED ABOUT COMMITTING TO REGULAR GIVING.

[a]It appears there were three different tithes required. One was to support the Levites (Numbers 18:21, 24); another was used to fund the feasts (Deuteronomy 12:17, 18; 14:23); and a third supported the orphans and widows (Deuteronomy 14:28, 29; 26:12, 13). The first two tithes were yearly, and the third appears to have been every third year.

to purchase something because you have committed your funds?

These are all real fears that believers face when God calls them to make a financial commitment. This also demonstrates why God is so serious about our finances. When you begin to examine the way a man spends his money, you are getting very close to his heart. But I have also watched young believers thrive as they cheerfully relinquish control in this part of their lives and begin to trust God for the future.

Sponsorships can be an excellent way to begin making small steps toward Kingdom giving. Just commit to give a certain amount for a period of time to a particular need. I recently talked to a young woman who lived with her parents and had very little income. She had committed to sponsoring a child for a year, and she shared what a blessing it had been for her. Due to her low income, there were times when she almost didn't have enough money to send in her payment. Sometimes she had to change her plans and give up activities to have enough. But looking back, none of this seemed a burden. The decision to commit had helped her see the blessing in regular giving. Her gaze was starting to shift from what her money could do for her to what God's money could do in His Kingdom.

As you consider committing to regular giving and you feel those tentacles of fear wrap around your heart, rest assured that Jesus knew exactly how we would feel. As you deal with fears of the unknown future, take time to read the words of Jesus. In the last half of the sixth chapter of Matthew, Jesus speaks to these very fears. Jesus knew we would have difficulty relinquishing control of our finances. But He is calling us to let go of the sofa and trust Him with every aspect of our lives.

First-Fruit Giving

In the Old Testament, God commanded His people to give of their first fruits. Each time they experienced an increase, such as at harvest, they were to give some back to the Lord. This served as a constant reminder of where these blessings came from. First-fruit giving provides an insight into the heart of God. He wants us to acknowledge His hand in every good gift. All of us experience times of increase. Maybe we are able to sell an item for more than we had thought, or we receive a raise or bonus at work. These are excellent times to show our thankfulness to God by giving a portion of the increase back to Him.

Give Sacrificially

Jesus seemed more interested in the size of a man's sacrifice than the size of his gift. As He watched the widow throw in those two mites, His assessment must have shocked the disciples.[b] We usually think the amount we give is the most important part. But Jesus said this woman had given more than all the rest, simply because she had given everything she had. Analyze your giving for a moment in light of this teaching. Are you willing to sacrifice to give? Sometimes our giving consists mainly of the unwanted and unneeded. It is not difficult to give money if we can't think of anything we need. There is no great sacrifice in giving time if it is spare time anyway. But are you willing to sacrifice to share? Can you consciously abandon something in order to give? Remember the widow and her two mites. We tend to focus only on what is given, but God's eye also looks at what is kept.

"JESUS SEEMED MORE INTERESTED IN THE SIZE OF A MAN'S SACRIFICE THAN THE SIZE OF HIS GIFT."

Give Quietly

Jesus gave us a method to analyze our motives: Are we willing to give unnoticed? If our hearts are motivated by love for the Lord, we won't mind if He is the only observer. It's not always easy to know our motives. It is easy to slip into a habit of doing or giving to be seen. But it is very important to practice giving quietly. Do everything possible to ensure that only the Lord is aware of your gift. However, there are times when it is impossible or even imprudent to hide what we are involved in. And it is possible to get so cautious about how things are done that very little gets done.

But Jesus knew our fleshly tendencies. He knew our tendency to de-

[b]Mark 12:43

sire praise and our "sanctified" ways of getting attention. The Lord has provided quiet giving as a way for us to analyze our motives and ensure it is His Kingdom we are primarily interested in building and not our own.

> IF OUR HEARTS ARE MOTIVATED BY LOVE FOR THE LORD, WE WON'T MIND IF HE IS THE ONLY OBSERVER.

This principle is very important. Learn to analyze events and activities not just by results, but in light of Scriptural principle. Many types of fundraisers can be effective and raise large amounts of money for good causes. But do they enable the donor to remain unnoticed? Is it possible that God is more interested in the principle than the amount of money raised?

Invest in the Kingdom

"Lay not up for yourselves treasures upon earth, where moth and rust doth corrupt, and where thieves break through and steal: But lay up for yourselves treasures in heaven, where neither moth nor rust doth corrupt, and where thieves do not break through nor steal."[c]

I don't think any of us totally comprehend the reality and potential of what Jesus said. I wonder how reluctant we would be to give if we could see what God has in mind for those who cheerfully invest in the Kingdom. Do you consider this truth when trying to decide how much to share? When you are deciding whether to purchase a nonessential item, do you ever picture what God could do with that money and what it could be worth in eternity?

Warren Buffet is one of the most well-known investors in America. He is famous both because he has made amazing financial decisions and because of his frugal lifestyle. In 1958 Warren purchased a modest stucco house in Omaha, Nebraska, where he raised his family. Now, one of the richest men in the world, he still lives where he always has, in one of the many houses in an American middle-class neighborhood. But the reason for his frugality should make us stop and think.

[c]Matthew 16:19-20

Warren Buffet understands the value of invested money. If you had let him invest $10,000 for you in 1964, your investment would have grown to around $80,000,000 by 2010. Buffet has always looked far down the road. Why waste money on a new Mercedes when that money could be invested and grow to tremendous value? Warren Buffet understands the potential value of investing and lives a frugal lifestyle so he can invest as much as possible.

But Jesus offered an even better investment opportunity that will keep paying dividends on into eternity. When Warren Buffet dies, all that he has ever accumulated will be worthless to him. He is one heartbeat away from losing it all. But the believer who has invested in the Kingdom is always just one heartbeat away, not from leaving his wealth, but from going to it.

> GOD IS BLESSING US TODAY, NOT TO INCREASE OUR STANDARD OF LIVING, BUT OUR STANDARD OF GIVING.

If you can grasp the amazing opportunity of investing in the Kingdom while you are young, you will be blessed in this life and in the one to come. I think heaven's rate of return is one of God's "little" surprises. God is blessing us today, not to increase our standard of living, but our standard of giving.

What if I Don't Make Enough Money to Give?

I have had people tell me they simply do not make enough money to give. Perhaps you have had thoughts like this as well. Maybe there are times when it seems there just isn't enough money to cover all your expenses, and giving seems impossible. Maybe after all your bills are paid and expenses met, there really is nothing left. Perhaps you have even gotten yourself into a financial condition where interest on credit cards and loans is eating up all your extra income, and you don't know where extra funds would come from. I don't know your situation. But before you decide to stop giving, here are a few questions you should consider:

- Are you currently spending money on any items not

needed for survival? (Soft drinks, cell phones, recreation, eating out, etc.) If so, could any of these items be abandoned to enable giving?

- If your income suddenly dropped 10 percent, would you go hungry? If not, would it not seem reasonable to share with those who are?

- Do you actually believe God is the one providing for your natural needs? Really?

- If your close friends, maybe those in your youth group, knew that you were not giving, would they agree that there is no way you can?

- According to United Nations statistics, about 25,000 people die every day of hunger or hunger-related causes. There is plenty of food in the world, yet someone dies every three and a half seconds. If you could explain to these people and their families why you are not able to share, would they understand?

- Many in our world today have never heard the Gospel. I remember sitting in a restaurant in China several years ago listening to a woman tell of her personal journey to faith. She was in high school before she even heard that there was a man in history named Jesus Christ. It would be many more years before she, through some miraculous circumstances, would hear more and come to a saving faith. This seemed incredible to me. This woman had not grown up in some little backwater village in a far-off province. She had grown up in downtown Beijing! Many who have heard something about Jesus have had no access to a Bible or teaching about the importance of living for Him. Could you give up a soft drink to provide a Bible to one of these people?

These statistics and questions are not intended to shame you or make you feel guilty. You did not choose where you were born. But you are living in a country of amazing opportunity, and you have some choices to make. Paul told the church at Galatia, "As we have therefore opportunity, let us do good unto all men, especially unto them who are of the household of faith."[d] I wonder if there has ever been a time with more opportunity!

Where Should I Give?

We have addressed the need for giving and the blessing of sharing, but where should you give? Since we have so much in our developed country, should all our money go to poorer countries? Should we always give to large organizations, or should we first help our local church, or try to personally find needs and give on our own? You must hold these questions up before the Lord and seek His guidance to find direction for your giving, but I would like to give you a couple of things to consider.

We believe our first responsibility is to our local church and the needs of our brothers and sisters in Christ. We do not want to neglect our church offerings to give to non-profit organizations.

Christian organizations can be a great blessing in reaching out to spiritual and physical needs around the world. They can accomplish things that we can't individually. But God wants us to do more than only support large organizations. Just sending a monthly check to an organization can become a crutch, and you may be missing something else God has for you. People all around you have needs. Look and pray for opportunities to bless and share with the hurting right around you. Sometimes, here in America, time is more valuable than money, and what is needed most is a listening ear. An active prayer life and a fervent desire to share the name of Jesus can reveal needs and unlock many local opportunities.

It is also important to analyze different organizations and their approach to aid. There is a time, such as after a disaster, to freely give out of love. These victims have lost their ability to provide for themselves, and our Lord would want us to give immediate relief. But other times ongoing aid

[d]Galatians 6:10

can actually hurt the people we are trying to help. When we continue to give aid to individuals who are capable of working, we may be doing damage. Does the organization you are sending money to understand this? As stewards of our Lord's goods, He expects us to share His resources wisely. This will require some thought, prayer, and investigation.

Conclusion

I don't know where you are with giving. Maybe you have been habitually sharing and living for the Kingdom. Perhaps you have already discovered the blessing in regular, sacrificial giving. Or maybe your giving has just been bursts of first-fruit giving—an occasional donation at a time when funds seemed unusually plentiful. Or perhaps you have been a conscience giver. You read about a disaster or read an article from some non-profit organization, look into the sad eyes of the forlorn child in the brochure, and your conscience begins to cause problems. Finally you break down and give to relieve the inner turmoil.

Or perhaps you haven't given much thought yet to giving. Wherever you are, I want to encourage you to step away from the comfort of the sofa. Go ahead and commit yourself to regular giving. Open your heart to the Lord in this area and let Him work. Spend time in prayer, specifically asking for guidance in giving. Allow the Lord to use your life as a channel of blessing. People with great needs are crying out to Him, and He wants to use your hands, feet, and checkbook for His glory!

For Further Reflection

1. God wants us to give cheerfully from the heart. So why did He require the tithe in the Old Testament? Why didn't He just let them give what they felt led to share?

2. What are some examples of first-fruit giving in our day?

3. Discuss the concept of giving quietly. How could some types of fundraisers violate that teaching of Jesus?

4. Discuss the fact that we spend money on insignificant items while many are hungry or need the Gospel. Which of these expenses could be eliminated or at least reduced in our lives?

5. Make a list of ways people invest in the kingdom of this world. Make another list of ways we can invest in the Kingdom of God.

Crosswinds | 18

IF ADVERTISERS SPENT THE SAME AMOUNT OF MONEY ON IMPROVING THEIR PRODUCTS AS THEY DO ON ADVERTISING, THEN THEY WOULDN'T HAVE TO ADVERTISE THEM.

—WILL ROGERS

One of the most exciting days during the process of getting my pilot's license was my first cross-country flight. I had received hours of training from my instructor, during which I had learned to be comfortable taking off and landing, mastered some basic navigational skills, and practiced how to respond in an emergency. I had learned to fly by myself, but primarily I had stayed close to home.

Now I was ready for my first solo cross-country flight. I was spending that fall in northern Indiana and taking lessons at Wabash Airport. On the morning of my flight, I went over the flight plan with my instructor. The plan was to fly from Wabash to a little town in the northeast corner of the state called Angola. We looked at the map together and drew a proposed flight path from Wabash to Angola. Every so many minutes along the way we also marked waypoints, places where I could visually ensure I was staying on course. This is a crucial part of a flight plan. Airplanes can easily drift during flight, and care must be taken to make sure the flight path is maintained.

I took off with a mixture of excitement and fear. There is something a little unsettling about heading out into the blue sky by yourself. But I was amazed how easy the flight was. With only minor adjustments along the way, I flew directly over the Angola airport. I landed briefly, had someone on the ground sign my flight log proving I had been there, and then prepared for departure. My flight instructor had told me that if things worked out well, I could try flying back using only my instruments. I had received very little training in the use of instruments, and I can only assume my instructor had an unrealistic confidence in my navigational ability.

I was in a cocky state of mind, given that the first leg of my flight had gone so flawlessly, and I decided to give it a try. But just a few minutes into my return flight, I became totally disoriented. I had confidently started off in the right direction, but the wind had increased, and I had been gradually blown off course. Due to my inexperience, the instruments did not work the way I thought they should, and as things on the ground started to look different than the map, I began to panic. Looking back, it was all very foolish. All the instruments I needed were right in front of me, but at the time it was pure terror. It is not much fun to be flying along with the sun going down and the fuel getting low, unsure of where you are going. Stopping in at someone's house and casually asking, "By the way, could you tell me how to get to Wabash?" just wasn't an option.

The flight worked out better than I expected. I happened to see a particular farm I was familiar with and realized I was not that far off course.

In the days before electronic navigational equipment, this type of dilemma was much more common. Stories abound of pilots getting lost in those early days. They would see a small airport on the ground, land their plane, and then casually walk around the local town, secretly scanning signs, anxiously trying to find a clue as to where they had landed. Crosswinds were a great enemy to those early pilots. Working ever so slowly, crosswinds had the capability of causing a pilot to unknowingly drift off course. Headwinds are a nuisance. They slow down progress and consume additional fuel. But crosswinds are the real enemy in navigation. They are subtle and often almost unnoticeable, but they can keep you from arriving at your intended destination.

Financial Crosswinds

We have looked at the importance of having a budget. A good budget is like the flight path on an aviation map. It maps out a path from where we are to where we want to be. We have also discussed the importance of knowing where we are going. Deciding to focus our lives and finances on the Kingdom is essential and is a daily choice in the life of a Kingdom Christian. But in this chapter we want to look at crosswinds.

Sometimes in a burst of zealous conviction we decide to commit our possessions, money, and all we have to the Kingdom. Maybe we even take the time to put together a budget and lay out just how we plan to get from where we are to where we really want to be. But as time goes by, we awake to the fact that we have drifted. Little by little we have departed from our original flight path. We have been caught in the crosswinds and have lost sight of our initial vision. Crosswinds are sneaky. Not everyone is affected by the same temptations, but I believe crosswinds affect all of our lives. Let's address some of the crosswinds that young people tend to encounter.

Crosswinds of Peer Pressure

One crosswind that is almost universal among young people (and older people as well) is peer pressure. We have a built-in desire to be liked. We want to belong, and sometimes it seems that the right clothes or car can help our social status. It is important to understand the impact peer pressure has on our lives. How many times have you purchased shoes or some type of clothing, not because your clothing had worn out, but because of how you thought it would appear to your friends?

This pressure can also come from our surrounding culture. We do not want to appear too weird when out in public. But usually the most powerful crosswinds come from our friends or youth group. We hear them talking about how certain types of clothing look ridiculous, or we hear our friends discussing how "cool" a certain item is. All of this can greatly affect our choices. We don't want to be the one who is different or the next focus of ridicule. Suddenly those stylish new shoes you thought were too expensive start looking very cheap. If buying those shoes can help you belong, spending that money can seem worthwhile.

But we need to understand that peer pressure is a chain. You purchase those designer shoes because someone else did, then another person buys them because you did, and the cycle goes on until someone has the courage to break the chain. We desperately need young men and women who will stand up against these chains of peer pressure. We need youth with enough love for the Lord Jesus that they are willing to look foolish for the Kingdom. If you can learn to overcome these chains in your youth, you will find blessing throughout your life. As you grow older, you will be tempted to succumb to similar pressures. But if you can allow the Lord to help you gain victory in this area while you are young, it will enable your relationship with the Lord to flourish and bring blessing in the lives of your friends.

Crosswinds of Advertising

It has been estimated that the average child growing up in an American home watches twenty thousand commercials every year on television.[1] It is no wonder our society is drowning in consumerism. Advertising is not primarily designed to address needs; it is designed to create wants. A good advertisement is supposed to take a man who is satisfied and make him discontented. Billions of dollars are spent in this attempt. Studies are done, human weaknesses explored, and advertisements created with the intention of exploiting our vulnerability. Marketing agencies go to great lengths to shape our thinking, and we foolishly allow them undue access to our minds.

One of the reasons we are impacted so heavily by the advertising world is the amount of access we allow. We cannot help seeing the billboards along the highway or the advertisements in the supermarket. But do we need to subject ourselves to continual temptation? How long can a woman continue to read *Better Homes and Gardens* and be content with a simple home? Can a man keep perusing *Car and Driver* every evening and still view his vehicle as only transportation? Think of applications in your own life.

> ADVERTISING IS NOT PRIMARILY DESIGNED TO ADDRESS NEEDS; IT IS DESIGNED TO CREATE WANTS.

If you are a young girl and continue to look through the latest beauty magazine, it will eventually affect the items you purchase and the way you look. If you are a young man and spend much time looking through *Field & Stream* or *Outdoor Life*, you can be sure it will affect your use of time and money. Feeding on this type of reading material will create a crosswind in your life that over time can blow you completely off course. Reading material shapes our world view. It helps us decide what is important in life. Continually reading hunting stories will cause you to view hunting as important. Spend enough time reading the financial pages of the newspaper, and eventually you will find yourself viewing everything that happens from a financial perspective.

But I believe even more powerful than magazines and newspapers is the use of catalogs for recreational reading. We sit down, tired after a long day. Our minds are weary, and we long for something to look at that requires little thought. Often our emotions are in escape mode. The job, the boss, the parents, the siblings, or

even the contrary coworker all bring stress into our lives, and we long to escape.

So we open a catalog pertaining to one of our hobbies. We gaze longingly at the pages as though we are peering into a different world. These folks do not look like the people we saw at work or on the road today. These people are all happy. Every one of them is smiling and enjoying life, and right there beside each joyful person is the product that is bringing them such bliss. Using these catalogs for recreational reading will stamp a thought process in our minds: people who have nice new things are happy.

Catalogs can be useful, but it is best to keep them in one place. Then when there is a legitimate need, we know where to go. But using them for recreational reading can be expensive and will encourage drift from our Kingdom path.

Crosswinds of Technology

Before dealing with the area of technology, go back for a moment and review the overriding vision for your life. What is it? Are you serious about using every resource God has given you for His Kingdom? Technology has an uncanny ability to blow you off your Kingdom flight path if you allow it to. It has the power to bring an amazing array of distracting sights and sounds into your life. It also can be a blessing if used correctly.

But right now let's examine technology simply for its impact on your time and money. In a study reported in *The New York Times*, the average teenager today is sending or receiving 2,272 text messages per month.[2] Texting has become an addiction with many teenagers, and the pressure to stay connected with friends is strong. Most of us feel insecure during this time of life, and the thought of being out of the loop is frightening.

In addition to the skyrocketing use of cell phones, researchers tell us that the use of all other types of electronic media is increasing rapidly as well. In fact, a report was recently released showing that young people between the ages of eight and eighteen years of age are using some type of entertainment media an average of seven hours and thirty-eight minutes a day.[3] That adds up to over fifty-three hours every week!

Much is being said today about the negative effects all of this is having on our physical and emotional health, our social skills, and our ability to think deeply beyond quick sound bites. But stand back for a moment and look at the effect it has on our pursuit of living for the Kingdom. How much time and money is going into entertainment that could be going toward the Kingdom? Maybe you are using electronic media only half as much as the national average. That still means three and a half hours a day are being spent with cell phones, IPods, or computers.

Can you get a vision for what could be accomplished in your community for the Kingdom in that amount of time? Are there older people in your congregation or neighborhood you could stop in and visit? Could you take food to a young family or help with tasks around their house? Are there any young boys or girls who could use some friendship? Maybe someone who does not have a stable father or mother who could use some direction? Could you be sending out a few notes of encouragement?

Then consider the financial drain this electronic media can be on our lives. Could the monthly fee you spend on your texting plan be used to sponsor a child somewhere? Do you really need to keep purchasing more music? Would those who are in need of more Bibles understand this use of funds?

We are inundated with enjoyable options. Most of them have some good, and most are not evil in themselves. But I believe having a clear Kingdom vision is our best defense against this onslaught. Satan is doing everything he can to distract you from your pursuit of the

Kingdom. Do not let him blow you off course with technology.

Crosswinds of Sports and Hobbies

Sports and hobbies are such powerful influences on our lives simply because they seem so harmless. We take strong measures to guard our lives against sinful activities and habits. We avoid going certain places and looking at certain things because the potential effect on our lives is obvious.

But the crosswind of sports and hobbies is so subtle and seemingly harmless that, almost without being aware of what is happening, our vision can gradually be shifted to something other than God. Suddenly we find ourselves with a stronger passion for a certain activity than we have for His Kingdom. I don't believe our Lord has in mind that we abstain from all hobbies or outdoor activities. Many of these activities can be a blessing and an enjoyable way to spend time with friends and family.

But I do believe these hobbies and sports, which have the potential to divert our attention from the Kingdom, should be viewed with caution. Many "harmless" things have the potential to steal our hearts and shift our overriding goal of serving the Lord Jesus. Jesus spoke about this tendency. He called it the "lusts of other things."[a] Our world is full of "other things" that can make us unfruitful. It will take a strong love for truth and discernment from the Holy Spirit to keep these "other things" from blowing us off our flight path toward the Kingdom. I have been blessed as I have witnessed young men and women with such a strong vision for serving the Lord that they forget about their hobbies.

> MANY "HARMLESS" THINGS HAVE THE POTENTIAL TO STEAL OUR HEARTS.

[a]Mark 4:19

Conclusion

Sometimes during a flying lesson the instructor will ask a student pilot to wear a special hood designed to allow him to see the instruments while preventing him from looking out the window of the plane. Looking out the window is not always an option. He may be in the clouds or flying at night. If he has never learned to depend on his instruments, it will be difficult for him to trust them in those situations.

A pilot needs to arrive at a point where he believes the instruments despite what he is feeling. I remember wearing the hood during a flight. We rely heavily on sight to remain oriented, and my brain told me the plane was tilting to the right. This feeling was strong, yet the instruments said everything was fine. A pilot must learn to ignore his feelings and trust his instruments. That isn't easy. It is very difficult to trust something other than feelings.

Our feelings are strongly influenced by our culture. Sometimes it just feels right to buy the latest cell phone, purchase brand-name clothing, and pour time and money into our hobbies. Something about sitting down in the evening and poring over the well-worn Cabela's catalog again feels good. But the Word of God tells us something different. The Bible tells us that our culture is heading in the wrong direction. If you are going to stay on course and ultimately land safely, it is vital that you focus on the unchanging Word of God and ignore the voices of our changing world.

For Further Reflection

1. Share a time when you felt pressured to purchase an unnecessary item. Can you identify the cause of the pressure you felt?

2. What are some ways we place temptations in our path by our choices of reading material? Can you think of catalogs and magazines that tend to shape your desires?

3. Discuss the impact technology is having on your age group. What are some positive ways it can be used? What are some uses of technology that can consume "our" time and resources?

4. List some projects youth in your church could be involved in that would bless your congregation or neighbors. Are there certain sports and hobbies that compete for your time and prevent these projects from blessing your community?

"They That Will Be Rich . . ." | 19

EARTH PROVIDES ENOUGH TO SATISFY EVERY MAN'S NEED, BUT NOT EVERY MAN'S GREED.
—MAHATMA GANDHI

They said it was a no-brainer. Only $35 and a small area inside your home to operate. The business was so simple that anyone could do it. All you had to do was mail $35 to Culture Farms. They, in turn, would send you an activator kit. You would take this culture activator, mix it with milk, and then wait for the concoction to work. After some time had elapsed and a film had formed over the milk, it was time to harvest. Just slip this film into a little bag provided by the company and send it back to them. The company would then take this valuable milk culture, process it into a wonderful skin cream, and mail you a check for your efforts.

It was so easy, people were saying, that a person had to be stupid not to get involved. With just a small amount of effort, you could turn a $35 investment into $900 in a few weeks. And imagine the potential if you purchased ten of these kits. You could change $350 into $9,000. Amazing!

I remember listening to those who were involved talk of this wonderful opportunity. It was so effortless, and best of all, it was working. One individual had been involved for only a few months, and already he had turned a couple of thousand dollars' investment into almost $50,000. Obviously, this was not a hoax. If Culture Farms was fraudulent, why would they be mailing out $50,000 checks? It seemed there must be a great demand for their product.

As new people got involved and started getting checks from Culture Farms, they told their friends, and more people sent in money for the kits. A few people in our community even charged the activator kits to their credit cards. After all, at the rate this milk culture investment was sending back profits, a check would come long before the credit card bill was due anyway.

But then it all crashed. Suddenly the checks stopped coming and the phone line at Culture Farms was out of order. Government officials had been warning people for some time that the scheme was fraudulent, but this only increased publicity and encouraged investors. Now the curtain was pulled back, and Culture Farms was exposed as a scam. The cultures people were harvesting and sending in were being processed and sent back out as starter kits for new investors. As long as there was enough revenue coming from new investors, Culture Farms flourished. But when federal investigators put pressure on the company to provide proof of their claims, the company folded. Investigators estimated that Culture Farms raked in close to $80 million from about 27,000 investors scattered across twenty states in the short time they were in business.

Every year millions of people fall victim to clever schemes like this one. These schemes prey upon human weakness and offer seemingly legitimate ways to circumvent God's method of working to provide for your own needs.

We could wish this topic did not apply to Christians. Surely followers of Jesus, who proclaim that this world is not their home, would not chase after easy methods of acquiring wealth. But unfortunately this is not the case. There are far too many examples of professing Christians getting caught in get-rich-quick schemes. As a young person intent on serving the Lord and using His resources for His service, it is imperative that you understand a little of why these operations seem so inviting. Let's begin by looking at how these swindlers operate.

Preying Upon Our Longings

"Earn $4,000 extra cash each month by working just a few hours a week at home!"

"Lose 30 pounds in 30 days while still eating what you want!"

"Reduce your credit card debt 70% instantly and legally!"

"Medical breakthrough! Natural juice discovered that cures many diseases!"

Such advertisements speak to our longings. After all, who wouldn't like to eat all they want without consequences, make a good living while staying at home, or find a new product that would eliminate medical struggles? We have a sneaking suspicion that others are not working as hard as we are , and we wonder if there is an easier way to make a living. Or maybe we find ourselves in debt. Life does not seem fair. Those credit card bills keep coming. The fees and interest keep adding up, and we secretly blame the credit card company. *Do they even have the right to charge this much?*

> WE HAVE A SNEAKING SUSPICION THAT OTHERS ARE NOT WORKING AS HARD AS WE ARE.

It's easy to get caught up in wishing things were different, and these longings and frustrations make us susceptible to scams. These fraudulent organizations devote time to understanding human longings and crafting programs that appeal to these desires. A basic understanding of how they operate can help you avoid their enticement.

Too Much for Too Little

One of the telltale signs of a scam is offering too much for too little. A swindler will seldom tell you his program takes hard work and a lot of time to produce results. Rather, you will usually be told this program takes little effort and results come quickly. Older and wiser people have said for many years, "If it sounds too good to be true, it probably is." This simple proverb can keep you from many potential frauds.

Sometimes it takes a few years, and a few mistakes, to understand that products are not usually worth more than their asking price. Fifty percent off may not mean it is a good buy. It usually means it was overpriced to start with. All of us like a good deal. We love the thrill of finding a product that is underpriced, and individuals promoting scams understand this instinct. Be suspicious when a company offers too much for too little.

I recently received a phone call from Bob. We were discussing financial struggles, and he shared an embarrassing situation he had been involved in. Bob had been reading a newspaper one evening and noticed an advertisement offering great income for simply stuffing envelopes. Bob said he felt a little sheepish from the start about pursuing the program, but it looked like easy money, so he sent in an application and the $20 fee. But he decided not to tell his wife about it. If it turned out to be profitable, he would reveal what he was doing, but if it didn't work out, she would never need to know.

So he had the package sent to his work address. Secretly Bob took the supplies home, and in the evenings when the rest of the family was asleep, he began to stuff envelopes for this company. The company sent a list of addresses and a pile of papers that needed to be mailed. He purchased the envelopes and postage, stuffed the envelopes, and mailed them to the addresses he had been given. After he had stuffed and mailed the envelopes, the company was to send him a check covering the cost of the envelopes and stamps and reimbursement for his labor.

One night as Bob sat down to stuff more envelopes, he suddenly woke up to what was happening. The letters he was stuffing in envelopes were exactly like the one he had received when he responded to the newspaper ad! All he was doing was getting more people involved in stuffing envelopes. But this wasn't the worst of it. Bob never received any reimbursement for the envelopes, postage, or time he had invested. All that was happening was that more and more people were sending in their $20, and the company was not even paying the postage!

Red flags should have popped up in Bob's mind when he read that a company was willing to pay lots of money just to stuff papers in envelopes. He should have asked himself some basic questions. Why would they pay that much for such an easy task? Why didn't they just hire someone to stuff the envelopes in their office? It makes no sense to spend money for advertising so you can pay someone lots of money for something that could easily and more efficiently be accomplished for less cost. If you can see no benefit for the company that is advertising, be suspicious.

Often these get-rich schemes sound so good and we want to believe them so badly that we fail to examine the facts and logic. Remember, if very little effort is needed and little time is required, a program will never need to be advertised. This world is full of people looking for big income with little commitment.

Let's look at another example. Advertisements are common in which companies offer high interest rates for the use of your money. Recently I saw an advertisement promising 20 percent interest if you let them borrow your money for six months. Stop again and ask, why are they doing this? If they are a reputable company, they can borrow money from a bank for about half that interest rate. Why would they pay you twice the interest? Being willing to ask a few questions can keep you from many financial snares.

THIS WORLD IS FULL OF PEOPLE LOOKING FOR BIG INCOME WITH LITTLE COMMITMENT.

Multi-Level Marketing

We have briefly looked at a few of the schemes being used by get-rich-quick promoters today. There are many more, and sometimes the products being sold are high quality. Often they use a sales program known as multi-level marketing. Multi-level marketing is a method of selling in which a salesman is compensated not only for what he sells, but also for sales that occur through the salesmen he recruits. For example, in traditional sales a man buys a product for $100, resells it for $125, and the extra $25 becomes his profit. This is how all the stores around us operate.

In multi-level marketing a man might buy a product for $100 and sell it for $200. But only $25 of that sale might be his profit. Another $20 goes to the man who originally got him involved in selling, and another $15 goes to the man who got *him* involved, and so on back the line. The primary focus in these programs becomes recruiting more salesmen instead of selling the product. Each new salesman is required to purchase his own product and then encouraged to have informal meetings with his friends to try to get them involved as well.

He will then make a profit on each sale they make. Friendships are exploited in this way and used in the pursuit of wealth. Setting up new dealerships is the primary path of growth for many of these programs, even more than personally promoting the product.

Before you get involved, carefully investigate the primary thrust of the program. Several years ago I became interested in a certain product. I talked to a sales representative and was invited to a meeting where a presentation was to be given. But I came away extremely disappointed. It was a multi-level marketing program, and even though the meeting had been called to present the product, the bulk of the evening was spent telling how selling the product could make you rich. Pictures were shown of boats and second homes. Stories were told of individuals who had been having financial difficulties. They had been introduced to this program just a couple of years ago, and now they didn't know what to do with all their money. The focus of the evening was on becoming wealthy and the virtues of financial independence.

Earlier we discussed the ongoing warfare between the god of mammon and the call of Jesus. The god of mammon says, "Life is about you. Enjoy this present world and get as much out of it as you can." The voice of Jesus encourages you to give up this present world. He warns you to ignore the materialistic calls that confront you and distribute to the poor. Now, in light of these two opposing voices, we need to ask a question.

Is the voice coming out of multi-level marketing the voice of Jesus,

or the god of mammon? Where is that inner urge to have the boat, to work less, or to own the second home coming from? There are good products being sold in some of these programs. But before you become involved, I encourage you to spend some time prayerfully answering these questions:

- Do I want to be identified with a method of marketing famous for dishonesty?
- Does Jesus want His followers to promote a focus on becoming wealthy?
- Do I want to be a part of a system known for overpricing and greed?
- Would the God of all truth want me to be known in my community as a person who uses friendship as a marketing tool?

Conclusion

If Jesus were here today, I believe He would weep at our misguided focus and passion. Why aren't we driven to share the Gospel the same way we chase after the latest health gimmick? Why don't we run to help our neighbor like we hurry to the next meeting on how to make more while working less? Why are we so tempted with each new product that promotes natural health, while we're seemingly so indifferent to spiritual vitality?

Having said all this, I am encouraged by what I see in many of our young people. I have witnessed some of them making difficult choices—decisions that cross their flesh as they turn their backs on this world and its values. As your generation begins to focus more on living for the Kingdom of Jesus Christ, change will come. I look forward to the day when, if time lasts, conservative communities are no longer known as places where get-rich-quick schemes are an easy sell—a day when believers are so passionate and focused on the Kingdom that the enticement of high living holds no attraction.

As the Apostle Paul instructed Timothy regarding the pursuit of wealth, he said, "But they that will be rich fall into temptation and a snare, and into many foolish and hurtful lusts, which drown men in destruction and perdition."[a] Chasing easy money can do all of this to our spiritual lives. But Paul went on, after giving more warning against the love of money, and said, "But thou, O man of God, flee these things."[b] If you are serious about living for the Kingdom, this is still good instruction!

For Further Reflection

1. Can you think of advertisements you have seen that offer too much for too little, or just sound too good to be true?

2. Can you think of individuals in your congregation who would be unmoved by get-rich-quick schemes? What is it that makes them stable?

3. Would your friends or coworkers say that your youth group's primary pursuit in life is the Kingdom of God? If not, what would they say it is?

4. List some steps you can take to protect yourself and others from the temptations these scams offer.

[a] 1 Timothy 6:9
[b] 1 Timothy 6:11

Consider Before Committing | 20

IT IS A GOOD THING TO LEARN CAUTION
FROM THE MISFORTUNES OF OTHERS.

—PUBLILIUS SYRUS

Even as I pushed the throttle forward, I had reservations. But with another airplane waiting impatiently behind me, I did not want to waste time going through the lengthy checklist. Prescott, Arizona, is known to be a difficult airport to depart from, and the fact that the runway was temporarily shorter due to construction made takeoff even more hazardous. The airport is over five thousand feet above sea level, and in the thinner air an airplane needs a longer runway to get airborne. So as I rolled out onto the runway with the four-seat airplane full of passengers, luggage, and fuel, I knew takeoff would be difficult.

I had given the plane a cursory inspection, pushed in the throttle, and was now rolling down the runway. But unknown to me, the engine was running on just one magneto. An airplane engine uses two spark plugs per cylinder. The magnetos power the spark plugs, so when only one magneto is in operation, the engine is not operating at its full potential. In my haste, I had failed to switch back to both magnetos, and now I was hurtling down the runway with too much weight, not enough runway, and insufficient power.

Anxiously, I began to watch the airspeed indicator in front of me. As I saw how slowly my speed was climbing, I became more concerned. This did not look good. The end of the runway was rapidly approaching. But at the last minute, with just enough speed, the plane gradually began to lift. I barely skimmed over the barbed-wire fence at the end of the runway. But though we were in the air, we were not gaining altitude the way we should have been.

Something was very wrong. I scanned the instruments, trying to discern the problem. Nothing appeared out of place, yet the lack of power continued to plague me. Finally, after what seemed like a very long time, I caught sight of the switch still pointing to one magneto instead of both, and the problem was quickly solved. With both magnetos in full operation, we had more than enough power and were able to continue our flight. But I could not help reflecting that we had narrowly escaped tragedy. Just a small oversight in aviation has the potential to transform a shiny airplane into scrap aluminum in seconds.

"JUST A SMALL OVERSIGHT IN AVIATION HAS THE POTENTIAL TO TRANSFORM A SHINY AIRPLANE INTO SCRAP ALUMINUM IN SECONDS."

All of this mental turmoil and potential grief was simply the result of failing to consider. If only I had taken the time to carefully go over my checklist. If only I had not been so concerned about the airplane waiting behind me and what others would think. But I didn't want to wait; I wanted to fly!

Many poor financial decisions are made because people neglect proper consideration. Perhaps we are walking through a store and see an item on sale. It looks nice, we have wanted one for years, and it is 50 percent off. We go ahead and make the purchase without proper consideration. We forget that our checkbook is low on funds, that additional expenses are due next month, and that we didn't even come into the store for this item to start with. We fail to consider the other places this money could have been put to better use. Now the money is gone.

But even worse than these small impulse purchases are the larger financial decisions we make without due diligence. I remember hearing a young believer lament a poor decision he had made several years before. The memory lingered because he was still making payments every month. He had been planning to move to an area known for mountains and snow. There wasn't much snow where he was moving from, and in the excitement of moving to this new mountainous area, he became interested in four-wheel-drive vehicles.

He did not waste any time. He found a truck he liked, obtained financing, and moved to his new home. Now, several years later, things look different. Recently he told me he would love to back up. "If only," he lamented, "I had taken the time to ask my dad before making that decision." His new job had not worked out quite as he had planned, living expenses in the new area were higher than he had anticipated, and the four-wheel-drive was not as necessary as he had thought it would be. The decision had been made in haste, but the resulting debt and financial frustration continued.

Our economy is driven by advertising and consumption. A tremendous amount of pressure is applied on the consumer, and the goal is to get him to purchase what he doesn't need. Time seems to be of utmost importance, and often we feel pressured into making financial decisions. We see advertisements proclaiming, "Sale Lasts Only Two Days!" or, "Hurry While Supplies Last!"

It is important to back up and understand marketing schemes. Be willing to ask some hard questions. If this store is really afraid supplies will not last, why are they spending all this money on advertising? What is the real purpose of this advertisement?

The answer is obvious. We don't think as clearly when we are rushed. The marketer is concerned that buyers will stop and consider before reaching for their wallets. Often the items being advertised are not necessities. If the consumer spends just a little time considering all the

WE FOCUS ON THE PRODUCT AND FORGET THE LONG-TERM PRICE.

legitimate places in his life he could use those funds, he probably will not buy.

Often, especially in our youth, we make hasty decisions that we regret for years to come. Like the young man who bought more truck than he really needed, we focus on the product and forget the long-term price. So let's look at a few steps we can take to ensure proper use of the resources God has placed in our care. They will help us avoid foolish decisions.

Purpose Not to Be Pressured

Resolve to take time when considering purchases. When you find yourself being pushed into buying quickly, stop and ask, "What's the hurry?" If the salesman applying the pressure really wanted you to be blessed by this decision, wouldn't he want you to take some time making it? Don't be afraid to take some time considering the purchase, investigating the product, and comparing other prices. If it is a long-term decision—if the purchase will affect your finances for a period of time—purpose to spend time in prayer over it. Just taking the time to hold the decision up before the Lord will help you avoid the snare of impulse buying.

Ask for Advice

Few things are more difficult in our youth than asking for advice. We are just breaking free from total parental control, and we want so badly to show others we understand how life works. But we never outgrow the need for advice, and wise men know how to ask the right questions.

When our children were young, I took them backpacking. After several hours of carrying my sixty-pound backpack up a steep mountain path, fatigue settled in. There were no road signs, and the children constantly asked, "How much farther do you think it is?"

Every so often we would stop under a tree, open our canteens, get the map out, and try to determine how far we had come. This was not always easy and sometimes was more of a guess than an intelligent calculation. Attempting to encourage them, I would say, "I think this might be the last major hill," or, "Maybe just around this corner we will see the crest of this mountain." But as the hills kept coming and one corner led to another, the children lost confidence in my navigational skills. What they really wanted was to meet someone traveling the opposite direction.

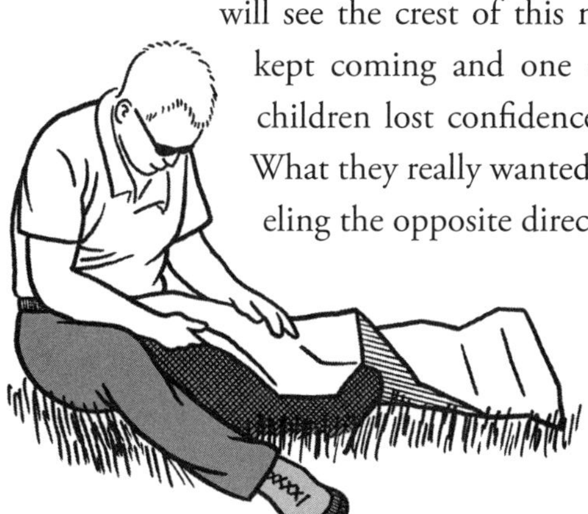

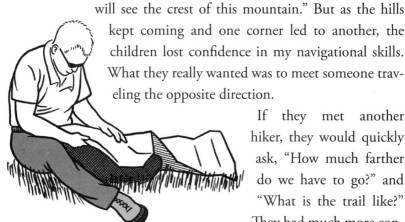

If they met another hiker, they would quickly ask, "How much farther do we have to go?" and "What is the trail like?" They had much more confidence in someone who had already traveled where we were heading. When you really want the best information, you ask someone who has already hiked this way before.

This same principle applies when making financial decisions. People around you have had experience. Your parents or grandparents may be the best resources to tap into when it is time to make decisions. But sometimes we forget. Sometimes we give more weight to our friends' opinions, even though they have little more experience than we do. So the next time you face a financial decision, take time to ask someone who has been on the trail longer.

> WHEN YOU REALLY WANT THE BEST INFORMATION, YOU ASK SOMEONE WHO HAS ALREADY HIKED THIS WAY BEFORE.

Use Kingdom Discernment

Auctions were rare in California, so when I attended one as a young man, I hadn't had much experience. It was all so exciting and happened so fast, and I couldn't wait to get in on the action. I went up to the table to get my number and then headed out into the crowd to participate. I watched for a while, saw how it worked, and then I spied the desk. It was a small wooden desk with several drawers, and I could picture exactly where I would put it in my room. I had no idea how much it was worth, but I got caught up in the bidding and ended up bidding $90 for it.

IT'S NOT A BARGAIN IF YOU DON'T NEED IT.

To this day, I have no idea why any other bidder would have bid $85 before giving up, but I still remember the feeling after the auctioneer hollered, "Sold!" It was a sinking feeling to suddenly realize I had invested a large percentage of my total savings in something I really had no use for. Yes, it would look nice in my room, but I did not need it.

Many of us are enticed by these types of situations. We see an item, get caught up in the excitement of the moment, and fail to consider if the item is really needed. That desk would have been a poor bargain if I had paid only $20 for it, because I did not need it. As you make financial decisions, remember: it's not a bargain if you don't need it. Therefore you will never know if that item is a bargain unless you use some discernment. Is it a need or a want?

Consider the Actual Cost

Often the purchase price is a very small part of the actual cost of the item. When I decided to pursue my pilot's license, I thought only about the price of training. But there are many ongoing costs associated with having a pilot's license. There are medical physicals, periodic flight exams, and the flying time required to keep your license current. Frequently renting airplanes to stay current is quite expensive. And besides the financial costs, there was the use of time. Being a good pilot requires time focused just on flying. There are airport updates to keep up with and newsletters to read and magazines to subscribe to. But when I originally considered becoming a pilot, I wasn't thinking about all of this. Many purchases in life are similar. Sometimes the original price becomes insignificant in light of the overall cost.

Think about the cost of storing all these items we take home. Forgetting to consider this cost is partly why so many American garages are full and our cars are parked outside. All of this stuff we keep dragging home has to be stored somewhere. I think about this every holiday season as I watch husbands stroll through the kitchen sections of department stores the week before Christmas. All those new gadgets are on display. A few years ago, about the only appliances on the store shelves were can openers, toasters, and coffeemakers. Today the scene has changed. The shelves display exotic bread machines, rice steamers, pineapple corers, and quesadilla makers. On down the aisle you can find French fry machines, salad spinners, and soda makers.

As I watch husbands calculate which new gadget their wives would appreciate, I wonder how many times these items will actually be used. How often will they make French fries or bring home a pineapple that needs coring? Do they really need a machine that will peel oranges? Are they really saving that much time? And what about the other costs? Do they really want to clean around a bread machine every day? Do they eat quesadillas often enough to justify taking up that much counter space? Sometimes I wonder if most of this stuff won't end up in the garage within a few months. It will get moved, swept around, and then finally end up in a garage sale to make room for more stuff next Christmas.

> "THERE IS BLESSING IN SIMPLE LIVING!"

Sometimes the actual cost is greater than the purchase price. We pay in lost time, storage, and maintenance for all the things we buy. Before you make that decision to buy, take some time to consider the actual cost to your life. There is blessing in simple living!

Make the Best Use of Funds

One final test I would encourage you to take before making that purchase is to ask yourself, "From God's point of view, is this the best use of these funds?" This is not always easy to discern. A purchase may appear like poor stewardship to others, but in your heart you really feel it is best. But other times you know a purchase is not really necessary and the money could be put to better use. I want to encourage you to ask this question while you are young. Make it a habit. Learn to run every financial question through this sieve. Is this really how God would want His money used? You will find this little exercise can have a dramatic effect on your life. Don't make this decision on your own. Ask God for help. If you are going to avoid being sucked into the materialistic culture around you, you will need commitment and Holy Spirit discernment.

Conclusion

Learning to take some time to consider before making commitments is not easy. This is especially true in our youth. Sometimes it seems our society, with its focus on materialism and instant gratification, is almost too powerful a current to fight. The flow of consumerism is so strong and the advertisements so persuasive that we find ourselves making decisions we later regret.

But I encourage you to start applying these Biblical principles while you are young. You will find as you get older that the current only gets stronger and the pressure increases. But if you can begin making financial decisions for the Kingdom now, you will find the battle much easier later on. Choosing to live for the Kingdom as you make smaller financial decisions now will establish a life pattern that will not only bless you, but will also increase your testimony for the Lord Jesus within your community.

For Further Reflection

1. Share some examples of times you have made purchases on impulse and later regretted the decisions.

2. Think of some items where the initial purchase price isn't really the main expense. What are some other "costs," not necessarily financial, associated with some purchases?

3. Discuss how we can determine if a purchase was a "good deal."

4. What are some steps we can take to avoid making poor financial decisions?

Selecting a Kingdom Chariot | 21

NO OTHER MAN-MADE DEVICE
SINCE THE SHIELDS AND LANCES OF THE ANCIENT
KNIGHTS FULFILLS A MAN'S EGO LIKE AN AUTOMOBILE.
—WILLIAM ROOTES

Two young men stood at the ship's rail and looked down at the crowd that had come to see them off. Their parents, church leaders, and the friends they had grown up with stood on the wharf as the old sailing ship pulled away from the dock. Only in their early twenties, the men knew they would probably never see their families and friends again. On this side of glory, their separation was permanent.

It had all started when their congregation had heard of a place in the West Indies called St. Thomas Island. On this island, they had learned, lived a wealthy British slave master who had brought three thousand African slaves to the island to work for him. This Briton hated religion. "No preacher," the master had emphatically declared in a public statement, "will ever stay on this island! If one is ever shipwrecked here, we will keep him in a separate house till he dies. We will not hear religious nonsense on this island."

This eighteenth-century Moravian congregation had discussed this terrible situation. Here were three thousand souls with no hope of hearing the Gospel! What could be done? Were these three thousand African slaves irrevocably doomed to hell because of one evil slave master? These two young men had listened intently as the older ones talked. Their hearts had been touched by the thought of three thousand men with no hope. They had talked of it, prayed about it, and finally made a life-changing decision. They had asked their leadership for permission to sell themselves as slaves. They planned to work with these Africans for the rest of their lives, sharing the Gospel as they worked.

Total Commitment

So as the ship pulled away from land, they knew they would never be back. This was not just a two-week mission trip where you went, took some pictures, and came back to tell others what you did. This was a lifetime commitment. They had sold themselves into a lifetime of slavery. They had laid their lives on the altar and would probably be treated worse than animals till they died.

As the ship moved farther out into the harbor, those on the wharf heard one of the men shout back to the shore, "May the Lamb that was slain receive the reward of His suffering!" It was the last they ever heard from the two men.

We love to read these types of stories. As young people, we want that kind of commitment in our lives too. These two young men counted the cost and decided to totally surrender their lives for the Kingdom. Could you do that? Would you be willing to walk away from everything you know, move to a distant island, and endure pain and suffering for the rest of your life? Would you do this so that the Gospel could be promoted? And would you be willing to do this without the admiration of others? It is one thing to go off to an island and then come back every year or so and receive accolades from those who stayed home. But could you do this without any human approval? Accounts like this cause something within us to burn. We desire that same level of surrender, dedication, and loyalty to God. Many young people among us today long for an opportunity like this—and it may yet come.

Which Is More Difficult?

But I think we should address another, more pertinent question. Is the scenario those boys confronted really more difficult than the challenges you face? Is it more difficult to move to an island for the rest of your life than it is to make Kingdom choices in the midst of a materialistic society? I do not mean to minimize the sacrifice of these two young men, but the question is not as simple as we might assume. I wonder how those men would do in our culture. I wonder how they would respond to the pressures and enticing offers you face today. That they were dedicated, there can be no question. But could they have survived the slow, subtle, self-centered influences of our society?

It is one thing to be willing to commit to Christian stewardship. It is another to let the Lord guide us as we make actual choices. In this chapter I want to look at one of the major choices you will face in your life—choosing a vehicle. This choice can be very difficult, especially for young men. We know there are better uses for our money than purchasing more vehicle than we need, but we struggle just the same.

Identify Your Goal

Sometimes I wonder if our families really need so many vehicles. In Honduras I stayed with a family of five who all shared a very old car. They could afford more vehicles, but they chose not to buy a second car. It took some planning to get the father to work, the two older children to different jobs, and use the car for errands during the day, but they made it work. One reason they were content doing this was because they were surrounded by others who had much less.

So do you really need a vehicle? Would there be a way you could share transportation with someone else?

Before beginning to shop, I would encourage you to sit down and give some thought to your goals in purchasing a vehicle. Why do you want to buy a vehicle? What are your needs? Is it primarily to travel to work? Is it just for social life? Are you picturing a gold-plated chariot? Something that will cause the common man to pause in mid-stride and admire? Or are you simply seeking basic transportation? What kind of vehicle does God want you to drive, and how much of His money should be spent on transportation?

WHAT KIND OF CAR WOULD GOD WANT YOU TO DRIVE, AND HOW MUCH OF HIS MONEY SHOULD BE SPENT ON TRANSPORTATION?

This simple exercise will accomplish two things. First, it will help you accurately identify your actual need from a Kingdom viewpoint, and second, you will have set a precedent for future decisions. This will not be the last major financial choice you'll need to make. You will find opportunities to approach financial decisions the same way in the future. After you have established what your actual needs are, you will be ready to move on to the next step.

What Are the Options?

Once you have decided what your real needs are for transportation, start considering available options. It's easy to reverse this process and begin looking at vehicles before identifying the need. But what type of vehicle would best fulfill your need? Which option will best help you reach your goals? Is an older vehicle available that would meet your needs?

Older Car?

I commonly hear several arguments when I suggest that someone purchase an older vehicle. Invariably they will say, "I'd like to drive an older car, but I'm afraid of all those expensive repair bills." Or, "I don't mind driving an older model car, but I really need dependability. I don't want to be left out along the road somewhere on my way to work."

Let's examine these more closely. Are there really justifiable explanations for buying a new vehicle? Before we look at the disadvantages of owning an older car, let's look at the price of buying new. Let's suppose you have $5,000 saved up for a vehicle and you decide to purchase a new one. The average price in 2011 for a new car was around $28,000. But let's say you find a car for $25,000 that will work for you. You put down your $5,000. After paying taxes, you will probably drive the car off the lot with a five-year loan for $22,500. If you have an interest rate of 7 percent, your payment will be about $426 a month.

With a new car it is easy to figure your annual cost. You just multiply the monthly payment by twelve. In this case it would be $5,112 each year. If you want to know the cost over the life of the loan, multiply your monthly payment times the sixty payments and then add in the $5,000 down payment. In this scenario you would have paid $30,560 for your car, which by this time is only worth about $10,000.

Now let's imagine another scenario. Suppose you decide to take that $5,000 and purchase an older car instead of using it for a down payment. There are plenty of older vehicles out there, and $5,000 can still easily buy a reliable car. Many cars are available in this lower price bracket simply because most of us don't want to be seen in them. We are afraid of the impact on our reputations.

A Living Sacrifice

But go back to the account of those two Moravian boys. Before they could get on that ship, they had to die to self. They could no longer be concerned about what others thought of them. They had considered the cost and willingly chosen to follow where Jesus was calling them.

Several years ago a young man in our congregation needed to buy a car. His job was about thirty-five miles from his home, so he was interested in finding a vehicle that could get him to work without using too much fuel. This young man was frugal and had a desire to be used by the Lord for the Kingdom. All he was after was transportation. After some shopping around, he found an old Honda Civic. The paint wasn't very good and the body had some dents; in short, there was no reason to lie awake at night fearing theft. It was just not a thing of beauty. The old Civic had a lot of miles on it, and because of this, he paid only $700 to drive it home.

For three years I watched him drive that car to work. He received some good-natured teasing about his old clunker, but he continued driving it until his needs changed. After he had sold the Civic and bought a vehicle that would work better for him with his new occupation, I talked to him about his experience driving the old Honda during those three years. He told me that, aside from general maintenance costs he would have had with any other car, his only major expense was getting the air conditioner repaired. This set him back about $200, and he was able to sell the car in the end for

$300. This means that his cost, besides fuel and normal maintenance, worked out to around $200 a year. With the number of miles he was driving a year, he spent a little over one penny a mile for depreciation and major repairs.

The average car in America today loses about 30 percent of its value in the first year. If this young man had purchased the new car we discussed earlier for $27,500 (after tax and title), he would have lost $8,250 in depreciation in the first year alone.[a] This works out to 45 cents a mile for the luxury of driving a new car that first year. Now, to be fair, we must admit it could have turned out differently. This young man could have needed to replace a transmission or engine. This would have changed the numbers, but it is still difficult to imagine a scenario that would have made buying a new vehicle justifiable.

Let's go back to the two options we discussed—the new car option with the five-year loan, versus purchasing the older vehicle for $5,000—and reconsider the arguments against buying and driving an older vehicle.

- **"Those repair bills really add up."** Do the math. Does the cost of repairs on these older vehicles really exceed the cost of a new car? In our example, the new car is costing you $5,112 each year. A rebuilt transmission on an older car might run $2,000—a huge outlay in one chunk, but far less than the $5,112 a year you would spend on new car payments alone. If you can't afford repairs twice a year, it's unlikely you can afford a new car payment every month. Another cost to remember is insurance. On a newer vehicle you will probably carry more coverage—and pay more

IF YOU CAN'T AFFORD REPAIRS TWICE A YEAR, IT'S UNLIKELY YOU CAN AFFORD A NEW CAR PAYMENT EVERY MONTH.

[a]This just means the car would have been worth $8,250 less than when he originally purchased it.

for what you cover—than with an older vehicle.

- **"I'm nervous driving an older car."** Maybe you tend to drive longer distances and reliability is a concern. But remember that even new cars are not immune to mechanical failure. Take some time to talk to your local mechanic when purchasing an older car. Often he can give you valuable advice and point out potential problem vehicles. Mechanical problems, especially when we are young, are more of an inconvenience to us than anything. And it's amazing how reliable some of these older vehicles really are.
- **"The repair costs more than the car is worth."** Sometimes we hear people say, "I'm not going to put that much into that car; that's more than the vehicle is worth!" But this is really very poor logic. We don't buy cars as investments; we purchase them for transportation. A $1,500-engine rebuild that keeps your fifteen-year-old Toyota on the road may still be a bargain if it enables you to drive it another couple of years.

WE DON'T BUY CARS AS INVESTMENTS; WE PURCHASE THEM FOR TRANSPORTATION.

The point here is not that everyone should drive clunkers for the Kingdom. Each person will need to evaluate his needs and prayerfully consider the options.

Some people are creative about their transportation. One idea that is becoming more popular is renting a vehicle for long trips. In other words, drive an inexpensive older vehicle locally and rent a car when you need reliability for a long drive. We tend to think of renting as being an expensive option, but if it enables you to drive a more economical vehicle the majority of the time, it may be a reasonable alternative.

Peer Pressure

When I selected my first car, I wanted something reliable. I wanted a vehicle that would last for a while and get good gas mileage. At least these were the criteria I stated to others. But deep inside I wanted something else. I wanted to belong. I wanted a vehicle that would express to others who I was. So as I looked at cars, I secretly examined each vehicle from this perspective. What would my friends think of this one? How would they respond if I drove up in that one?

Which one should I drive?

I have talked to many young people since then and have found that I was not alone. Many young people are so driven by peer pressure when purchasing vehicles that they end up not only spending more than they should, but committing to loans that affect them for years to come. I have worked with several young families who are still trying to recover, years later, from poor financial decisions made in their youth.

Most of us probably agree that peer pressure is a powerful influence in our youth, and it greatly affects the vehicles we drive. I want to encourage you to discuss this in your youth groups. Don't let Satan continue to divert a large quantity of money that could be used for the Kingdom into vehicles. Your friends need to hear you say that it's okay if they drive less expensive cars. Watch for opportunities for good spontaneous discussions on this topic—times when everyone can share his desire to use every resource we have been given for the Kingdom. If you can do this, you can effectively relieve the pressure many of your friends are feeling.

Conclusion

The Apostle Paul, while describing the battle of life, told the church at Corinth, "I die daily."[b] I think we understand what he meant.

[b] 1 Corinthians 15:31

Every day he needed to again make a conscious choice to die to himself so he could live for Christ. That was not easy. Death never is. But I suspect we underestimate the subtlety of our culture and the need to die to our selfish desires. We understand the big battles. The sins of lust, murder, and stealing we understand and fight. But too often we forget to keep our armor up in the area of covetousness and materialism.

> WE UNDERESTIMATE THE SUBTLETY OF OUR CULTURE AND THE NEED TO DIE TO OUR SELFISH DESIRES.

I think it would have been easier for the Apostle Paul to submit to dying at the stake than to continually choose to die each day. We are in the same place. Choosing to head for St. Thomas Island as a slave would be quite a commitment. But I wonder if living out a Kingdom commitment in the area of personal finances is any easier. Perhaps it is easier to die on St. Thomas than at the car dealership.

For Further Reflection

1. Discuss the illustration in the beginning of the chapter and compare martyrdom with the subtle battle against materialism. Is one more difficult than the other? Why or why not?

2. If someone in your youth group chose to purchase an older car, what would you think of him?

3. From a Kingdom perspective, what should be the important points to consider when buying a vehicle? How important are style, age, color, maintenance records, make, model, etc.?

4. How much regard do the young people in your setting give to others' vehicles? Do you feel pressured to spend more than necessary? If so, how could this pressure be reduced?

Consumer Credit and the Kingdom | 22

THE RICH RULETH OVER THE POOR, AND THE BORROWER IS SERVANT TO THE LENDER.

PROVERBS 22:7

Several years ago an advertisement went out offering a free Dell laptop computer. There was an asterisk beside the offer, but thousands of young people responded. In fact, at the time I read about it, over 75,000 people had already signed up.[1] According to the offer from Universal Savings Bank, all you needed to do to receive your "free" Dell laptop was to sign up for their Platinum Visa card and either transfer a $5,000 balance from another card or take a $2,500 cash advance from them. Of course, in the fine print there were a few other details. (Isn't the real story always in fine print?)

The advertisement said you must keep a $3,500 balance on the card for at least eighteen months. If you failed to do this, you would be charged a one-time fee of $600. Of course, in addition to this fee, you would be paying interest along the way. If you did everything correctly (they hope you don't) you would pay about $600 in interest alone during this eighteen-month period. So for $600 you could receive a "free" computer which was available online at the time for about $500.

Our newspapers and mailboxes are flooded with "amazing" offers we would do well to view with skepticism. The flyer for this credit card offer said, "There has never been a credit card offer quite like the Universal Savings Bank Upfront Reward Visa Platinum offer." This statement is probably correct. But are offers like this, which encourage more consumption and debt, really a blessing to us? Will credit cards and consumer debt help us in our goal of living for the Kingdom?

Credit Card Chaos

Credit card use among youth is very high. It is estimated that 30 percent of high school seniors and 78 percent of college students are using credit cards.[2] As the percentage of credit cards has jumped, so has bankruptcy among youth. Before 1995 only 1 percent of bankruptcy filers were under twenty-five years of age. But by 2007 the American Bankruptcy Institute reported that 19 percent of those filing for bankruptcy were college students.[3] Easy credit has swept this country, and unless you understand the dangers, it is easy to be swept along with the current.

Credit brings with it an illusion. I worked with a young man years ago who had gotten himself into credit card trouble. Jim had a good job and a nice car, and he always seemed to show up with new shoes or a new jacket. Somehow he could always afford the latest. Everyone liked Jim, and no one suspected that he had financial problems. One evening Jim stopped in to visit. In the course of conversation, he began to share his financial struggle. No one could have told from the outside, but Jim was in trouble. He was living a lie and was miserable. He knew the day would soon arrive when his friends would discover his secret. Almost everything he owned had been purchased on credit. His car, his clothes, and even his trips to Pizza Hut had all been financed by his credit card.

Now as the interest accumulated and his balance continued to climb, Jim was scared. This had been fun at first. He could go anywhere and do anything, always assuming he would pay that card off later. But later had come, and he did not know what to do. Debt can provide an illusion for a while. You can hide behind the car and the clothes—but only for a limited time.

Things Are Not What They Seem

I spoke with a bank teller a few years ago who told me one of the most interesting parts of her job was comparing the computer screen, which told the facts, to the appearance of the person she was helping. Some people would come in looking like millionaires. From their styled hair to their classy shoes, it was obvious they had loads of money. But the computer screen told a different story. It showed very little in their accounts and sometimes a heavy debt load. Others would come wearing older clothes, yet they had high balances in their savings accounts and no debt.

America is a land of illusions. Perception is everything. You can give an appearance of wealth while actually possessing very little. Marketers promote this, and people are encouraged to buy now and pay later. Credit card companies have also encouraged this instant gratification. They have taught consumers to believe that making small monthly payments after you have taken the product home is easier than slowly saving before purchasing.

Credit Illusions

But those who are wise will stop and ponder this proposal. Is this really easier? Is it really better to buy a product before you can pay for it? Or is this simply an illusion? We are susceptible to illusions. Look briefly at the illustration below and quickly determine which of the people is the tallest.

Probably your first response would be that the people on the right are taller. But if you keep looking at it for a while, you will see that all four people are actually the same height. The perception in your mind exists because of the building drawn in the background. The background becomes our point of reference, and we judge the size of the people by this reference. Illusions are very effective when we don't take the time to consider. This is also true when purchasing with credit. Very few people would fall for many of the marketing ploys out there today if they simply took a little time to prayerfully consider.

Marketers have used credit for years to create an illusion. Like the illustration, they try to persuade us that things are different than they are. You thought you needed to pay money to take that new sofa home, but the sign says you can take it with you today, even if you don't have any money with you. You had always been told not to make car payments because the interest is so expensive. But this advertisement says you can drive a new car off the lot and "Pay 0%* interest." All of this sounds so good, but a little basic understanding about marketing and credit can save you a lot of pain. And don't forget the importance of those little asterisks.

How Do Credit Card Companies Make Money?

Let's look for a moment at how credit card companies operate. How do they make a profit? Remember, that is why they are in business. They are just like every other company out there. More money has to be coming in than going out, or they would be out of business. They obviously provide a service, employ many people, and make money, so how do they do it?

- Various fees. This would include annual fees for the privilege of having the card, as well as charges for not obeying the rules. Sometimes these "small" fees are not so little. It is not uncommon for credit card holders to be charged hefty fees just for sending in their payment a few days late. These late fees are a major portion of credit card companies' total income.

- Interest on credit balances. Interest is another way these companies produce income. When you are not able to pay off your balance at the end of the month, they charge interest. These interest rates vary from 7 percent to 36 percent, with the national average currently at 16.74 percent.[4] This is a higher rate of interest than most banks charge, so credit card companies profit from this as well. But remember, these companies are taking a large risk. They are trusting with no real promise that people will pay back their loans, so if you are paying interest, you are also helping pay the loans of people who default on their debts.

- Merchant charges. The stores you purchase products from must pay a small percentage to the credit card companies for the privilege of providing this service to their customers. This small fee usually ranges from 1 to 4 percent of each purchase. This means that when you go into your local store and charge $100 on your credit card, that store only receives $96 to $99 from the credit card company. The credit card company pockets the balance.

- Using their connection with you. Another source of income, which has been decreasing due to new regulations, comes from the company taking advantage of its relationship with you. Many advertisement companies are willing to pay to receive information regarding potential customers. For example, suppose you have a Cabela's credit card. Can you imagine how many other sporting goods stores would like to have your name and number? Credit card companies often sell their lists of customers to advertisers, and this becomes a source of income. In addition, sometimes a monthly bill from a credit card company will include advertisements from other companies. These other organizations pay the credit card companies for the right to use their monthly billing as a way to reach more customers.

How Do Credit Cards Create an Illusion?

Earlier we discussed the fact that credit card companies attempt to create some financial illusions. Credit card companies, like all other companies, need customers. Their product is credit, and somehow they have to convince you that you need their product. Let's look at a few illusions these companies provide to persuade us to use their cards.

The Illusion of Instant Gratification

In years past your grandfather needed to occasionally buy things just as you do. If he needed a piece of furniture, for example, he probably saved his money. Little by little, he accumulated the needed cash until the day finally arrived when he had enough to purchase the furniture Grandma had been wanting.

Credit card companies have gone to great lengths to convince us things are different now. The focus of consumer credit companies is instant gratification. Saving, they insinuate, is a historical process no longer in vogue. Not only should you have what you want, they tell you, but you should have it now. And more than that, you *deserve* to have it now!

We like the sound of this, and coming right on the heels of this great offer is a "no pain" promise. Marketers use this pitch in their commercials and promotions. We see advertisements proclaiming, "No payments for six months, same as cash!" This type of marketing particularly appeals to young people, and these companies spend millions of dollars focusing their advertisements on youth.

> NOT ONLY SHOULD YOU HAVE WHAT YOU WANT, THEY TELL YOU, BUT . . . YOU DESERVE TO HAVE IT NOW!

The Illusion of Wealth

A Dunn & Bradstreet study recently found that people spend 12 to 18 percent more when using credit cards than when using cash. And McDonald's found that the average transaction rose from $4.50 to $7 when customers used plastic instead of cash.[5] While these statistics may be skewed because people tend to charge larger transactions and use cash for small ones, other studies have confirmed that our purse strings tend to loosen when using plastic.[6] Why is this? Why do we tend to spend more when using credit cards than we do when using cash?

Each person's experience may be different, but I have found there is less pain when swiping a card than when using cash. Somehow I tend to equate cash with hard work. Consider this before moving into credit cards. Something about carrying around a credit card with a $2,000 spending limit makes us feel as if we have $2,000 just waiting to be spent. But having a card that enables us to immediately purchase something does not actually mean we have more money. This feeling is an illusion.

The Illusion of "Tomorrow Will Be Better"

Young people are generally optimistic by nature. This is a good trait when focused in the right direction, but can cause severe problems in finance. It's a great feeling to be young and have life before you. The world looks good and the future bright. There is a certain optimistic feel in the air. So many young people are shocked to discover, just as they are ready to go out and make a purchase, that there really is no money in the account. They know they are making a good wage, and it doesn't seem as if they have been spending that much. But the fact is they are out of money. At that point there is a tendency to assume this dilemma is unusual—to suppose that life will soon have fewer problems and tomorrow will be better.

To illustrate this, let's consider a young man named Fred. Fred works for a local farmer and has never worried much about finances. He hasn't really needed to worry, since he lives at home and his only expenses are his pickup, his hobbies, and going out to eat with friends. Recently, Fred signed up for a credit card. He had several reasons. First, you never know when an emergency might come up, and second, he had heard it was good to have a credit card. Something about helping your credit score, they said. But last, and probably most important, he could earn points on this card and eventually get free gifts at the local sporting goods store.

Harvest is almost over now, and all the other boys are preparing to go deer hunting. Every time they get together, hunting is the talk—the best location, which type of tree stand works the best, and, of course, what kind of rifle is best suited to the job. Fred listens to all of this and becomes increasingly aware that his dad's old rifle is not quite up to par. In fact, when the boys ask him about his gun, the topic is embarrassing. So Fred stops in at the local store and looks at the new rifle the boys have been discussing. There's no question. It is nice! It comes with a scope and is just what he needs. The only problem is the money. It costs $475, and Fred is a little low on funds.

He really doesn't want to use his credit card. He had decided to use it only in an emergency. But he really "needs" that new rifle. After seeing it, he realizes that Dad's old one really is out of date. This rifle is clearly far superior. Also, Fred reasons, if he uses his credit card, he will begin earning those points. This will put him on his way to getting other items he needs free.

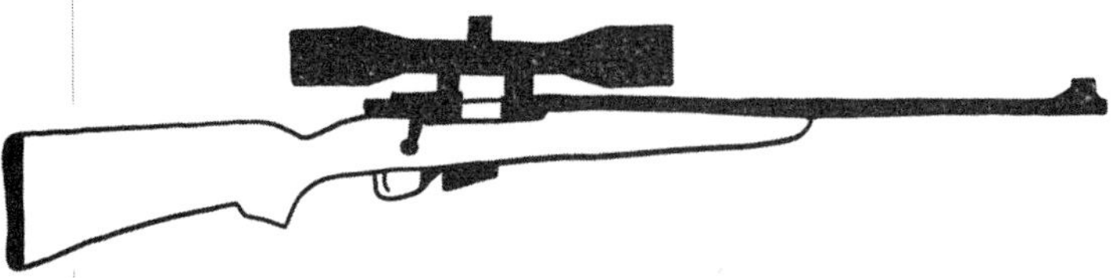

But there is one more reason Fred decides to charge the rifle: Fred cannot see the future. He doesn't know that his pickup's transmission is going to go out next month. He does not realize that he will need to use his card again to pay the repair shop, and that consequently it will be several years before both the rifle and the transmission repair are paid for. Fred just assumes that tomorrow will be better.

Many young people get started in credit card debt just like Fred. I have never yet heard anyone say, "Well, I just decided to get involved in credit card debt." No, it all starts very innocently, but life keeps bringing challenges. Once you cross the line of assuming tomorrow will be better, you have placed yourself in a position of great vulnerability.

The Illusion of Rewards Programs

Many people use credit card programs that offer rewards. Some of these programs can be beneficial. If you have a business, for example, where you can pay for a high volume of supplies on a credit card and earn air miles at the same time, this can be advantageous. However, for many people using these programs, the reward is an illusion. The typical reward on these cards usually has a value of 1 to 3 percent. This means that for every $100 you charge on the card, you will receive $1 to $3 back in rewards. But as we discussed earlier, the average consumer tends to spend 18 percent more when using a card instead of cash. So if you are like most people, you will end up losing money by receiving "free" gifts.

Another thing to remember when using these programs is the miscellaneous fees you get stuck with throughout a year. All it takes is just a few times of sending your payment a day late, or even having your payment get lost in the mail, and those extra charges can make those free gifts very expensive. These programs can be an illusion.

> SO IF YOU ARE LIKE MOST PEOPLE, YOU WILL END UP LOSING MONEY BY RECEIVING FREE GIFTS.

Debit Cards

Many people use debit instead of credit cards. A debit card automatically withdraws money directly from your checking account, making it more difficult to spend more than you have. However, there are a couple of things to consider when using debit cards. One of the problems is not being able to remember how much you have spent. I would encourage you to use a checkbook register when using a debit card. Writing it down can help you spend carefully and keep track of where you are throughout a month. The other thing to consider is that it is still easier for most to spend with a debit card than it is with cash. You may find yourself buying things with a debit card that you would not have purchased with cash.

We live close to a university, and recently I stopped in to pick up some clothes from the dry cleaner across the street from the school. As I paid my bill, I asked the lady at the counter if many of the university students brought clothes there to be cleaned. She said many of the students did bring their clothes there, but one thing she could not understand was why they brought their hand washing in. The shop charged $9 to wash a girl's top, and all these girls would have to do is wash the tops in their bathroom sinks and hang them up to dry. But she had concluded the problem was that they paid with their cards and were not even looking at the cost.

This tendency is one of the dangers in using either credit or debit cards. Cards tend to psychologically isolate the consumer from the cost. This is wonderful for the seller, but hazardous for the buyer.

"CARDS TEND TO PSYCHOLOGICALLY ISOLATE THE CONSUMER FROM THE COST. THIS IS WONDERFUL FOR THE SELLER, BUT HAZARDOUS FOR THE BUYER."

Conclusion

In the book *The Science of Self-Control*, researchers placed pigeons in a cage.[7] In this cage were two buttons, one red and the other green. At certain times throughout the day, these buttons would light up. When a pigeon pecked at these illuminated buttons, a portion of feed would be dumped into the pigeon's feeding tray. When the green button was pecked, one ounce of feed immediately dumped into the tray. But when the red button was pecked, two ounces dumped into the tray after a waiting time of four seconds. In other words, the pigeons would receive more food if they were willing to wait. They found that nearly all pigeons, when given the choice, will choose to receive the feed immediately, even though they receive less.

Credit card companies have proven that we are not a lot smarter than pigeons. Too often we are not willing to wait. Even the unbelieving world understands the dangers of credit cards and the potential they have to create illusions in our lives. But for those of us who desire to build the Kingdom of Jesus Christ, just refraining from using credit cards is not the solution. The greater problem is the desire that drives us to use them. May our desire to assist the poor, to reach the lost, and to build within the Kingdom be so strong that we are unaffected by the latest trinkets and illusions.

For Further Reflection

1. List some ways people use consumer debt to portray themselves as successful.

2. Share a time when you were content with an item you owned until you saw someone else with something better.

3. How can we avoid putting pressure on others? How can we encourage others toward contentment?

4. Make a list of comments we make that reveal that we view appearance or style as important. What comments would encourage contentment?

Saving and Serving— A Window of Opportunity | 23

IF YOU CAN'T FEED A HUNDRED PEOPLE, THEN JUST FEED ONE.
—MOTHER TERESA

"I just wish I could back up in time," she said. "There are so many things I would do differently!" As I listened to Katie and her husband Bill, my heart went out to them. Katie was a young mother of several children, dealing with all the mundane tasks young mothers face. As Katie and Bill discussed their finances with me, they suddenly began seeing that brief period of life before marriage in a different light. Those days were gone now, and they looked different in the rearview mirror.

"We wasted so much time and money during those years," Bill continued. "We didn't really do anything bad, but all we were thinking about was having a good time. I wish we could just back up and relive that period of our lives."

But although life comes with many features, it does not come with reverse. Often we long to back up. Suddenly we realize we have failed to properly use or enjoy a period of life we will never experience again. Sometimes in the insecurity of our teenage years we long for those times past when we could just hold our parents' hands. We found safety and comfort there, but those days are gone. Some of us who are parents wish we could back up and spend more time with our children, but we can't. Life just keeps moving.

ALTHOUGH LIFE COMES WITH MANY FEATURES, IT DOES NOT COME WITH REVERSE.

Bill and Katie were experiencing this same feeling. They had spent their teenage years living from one enjoyable event to another, like jumping from rock to rock across a stream. There had always been another exciting trip or function on the horizon. Of course, there had been those valleys of disappointment, those times of rejection and insecurity, but another exciting event would soon come along, and they were once again excited and moving forward. Even though they really had not thought about it during those years, their lives had revolved around themselves. Now all of that was over.

Time and Money

During those years, they had an abundance of time and money. Now they were painfully aware that they had not used those resources as they should have. They had now entered a period of life when both time and money were scarce, and they realized they would never have the same opportunity again.

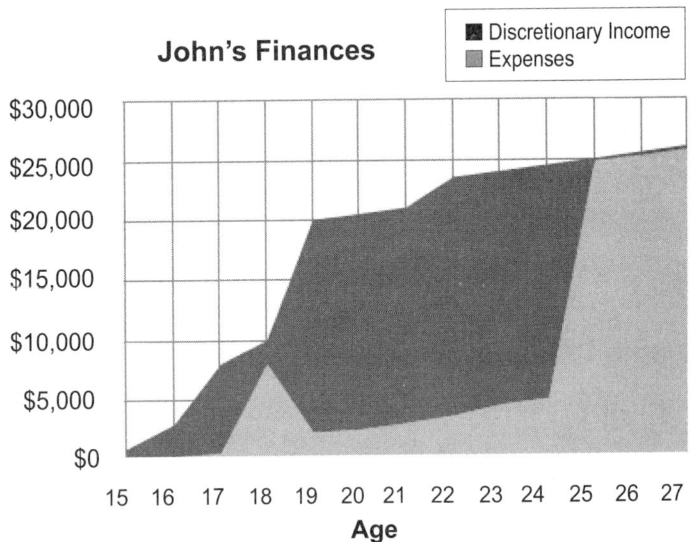

Earlier we looked at the hypothetical life of a young man named John. We looked at this chart of his financial life between the ages of fifteen and twenty-seven and considered how he might have used his discretionary income before marriage. But now we want to look at this brief time of youth from another perspective. We want to continue with John and examine what this graph might look like at the end of his life.

Let's imagine that John continued to work for Quality Electrical, and over the years his wages continued to increase. As you can see on the chart below, by the time he was forty, he was earning about $45,000 each year. His income continued to climb during the next twenty years as his experience became more valuable to the company. Finally, at the age of sixty-two, John began to slow down. He began to spend less time at work, and then, due to declining health, his income dropped rapidly. By the end of his life at seventy, he was earning about $30,000.

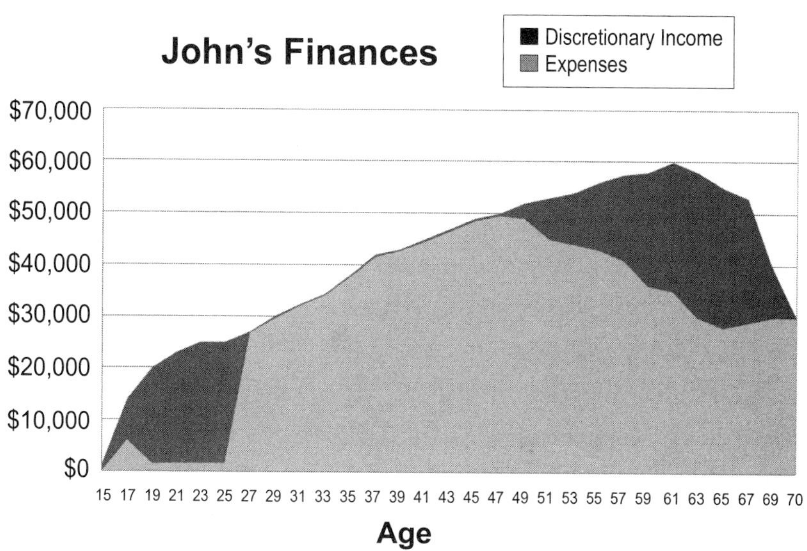

As you look at this graph of John's financial life, you can see that his expenses changed as well. From the time John was married until he was almost fifty years old, there was very little extra money available. During this twenty-five year span there were many expenses. Paying off the mortgage on their home and the many costs associated with raising a family consumed almost all the income John brought home. But about the time John turned fifty, things began to change. The last payment was finally made on the mortgage, and some of the older children began to move away from home. These changes greatly reduced John's expenses. For the first time in many years, he had a significant amount of money that was not allocated for anything. For the last twenty-five years, many needs had always been crying out for every dollar John brought home. But now things were different—and yet somehow vaguely familiar. When John turned fifty, he entered a time similar to his years as a teenager.

There are two periods of time in the average person's life when there is an abundance of discretionary income. One is later in life, when expenses begin to drop. But the other, and the time we are focusing on in this book, is during those early years. Most young people do not realize the tremendous opportunity they have during their youth. It is tempting to waste both time and money during those years, and the burden of this chapter is to encourage you to consider the great opportunity that is yours. As we consider this, let's look at Sam and Emily's situation.

It was only a couple of months until Sam and Emily's wedding, and as I sat down with them in my office, I marveled at their foresight. I didn't know either of them very well, and when they called, I wondered what they wanted to discuss. Most young couples give little thought to money until there is not enough, but as I soon found out, Sam and Emily were an exception. Both had taken their youth seriously, and both had quietly been saving for marriage. Together they had a sizable amount in savings and wanted some advice as to how they should begin planning financially for their coming married life.

But they were concerned about more than just saving. Sam and Emily had used these years in their youth to bless others. Their time, and some of their money, had been shared. They had found joy in living for the Lord as singles, and now they wondered how to continue using their lives to bless others after marriage. They were concerned that in the busyness and stress that accompanies starting a new home, this vision would be lost.

Saving and Serving

I want to encourage you to view the time you are in as an opportunity to both serve and save. This part of life can be wonderful. It can prepare you for a fulfilling life of Kingdom building and be a time you can look back to with joy and good memories. Let's look for a moment at how saving and serving during your youth can be a blessing throughout your whole life.

Saving

One comment frequently heard from young people after marriage is, "I wish I had saved more." I have never yet heard a young-married man look back over his youth and say, "I sure wish I had spent more on hunting equipment while I was young." I have never heard young couples lament, "If only we had driven nicer cars." No, the almost predictable comment is, "Why did we waste so much money on things that didn't really matter?"

> I HAVE NEVER HEARD YOUNG COUPLES LAMENT, "IF ONLY WE HAD DRIVEN NICER CARS."

George was a young man who worked for me years ago. He was diligent, prompt, and worked well with the other employees. But George, like many young men, gave little thought to the future. As his paycheck came each week, there were always plenty of things he "needed" or trips he wanted to take that consumed his check. So his financial life just bounced along from check to check.

At the end of every year the government requires that each employee receive a W-2 form stating how much they earned during the previous year. It was always interesting to see employees' responses as they received their W-2s . Some of them knew where they were financially, and their W-2 contained no surprises. But others were shocked at how much they had earned. They had no idea they had received so much during the previous year.

I still remember the phone call I received from George after he opened his W-2. He called to let me know there had been a mistake on his income. He was positive that he had not earned anywhere near the amount this little paper was saying he had. In fact, he was so sure, he asked if I would drive over to the office that night and get this straightened out. So I met George at the office, and we went back over his income for the year. There was no mistake. He had earned far more than he had imagined. But as this realization settled in George's mind, another question arose. Where had all that money gone? As we talked that evening and looked back over the past year, it became painfully obvious that almost all of his income had been spent on things of no lasting value. It was a painful and sobering lesson for George, and he began to take life more seriously from that day forward. George learned that, over time, an amazing amount of money can be wasted on pizza and parties.

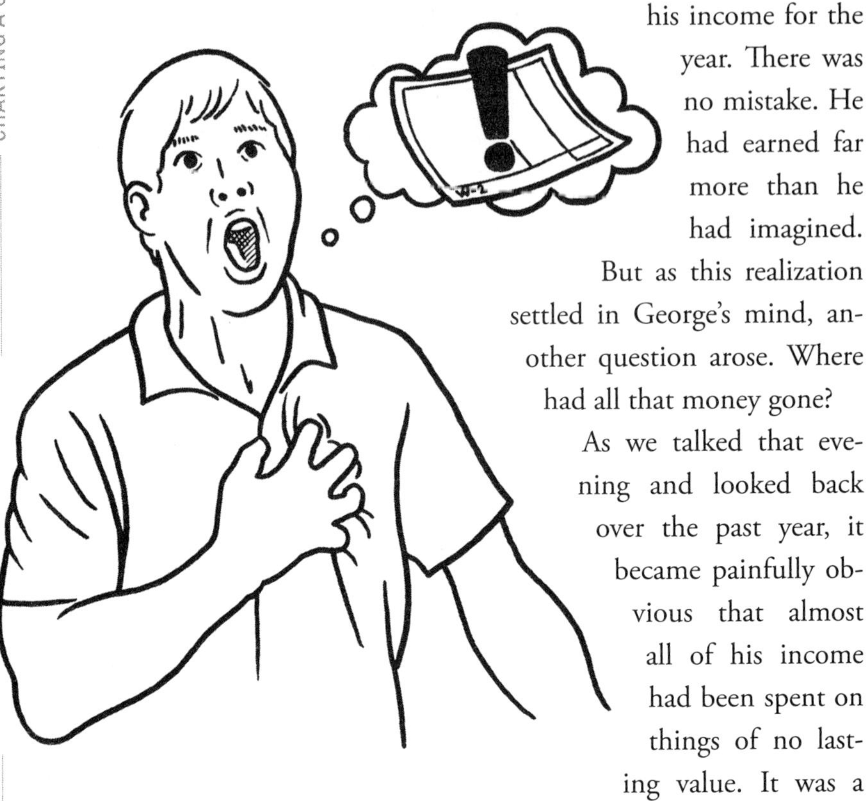

But these years do not need to be wasted. These years of living at home can be a wonderful time to prepare for life. It's a time when you can look down the road and save for large expenses on the horizon—future expenses like homes or starting your own business. These years can be a blessing, and if they are used wisely, you can look back on them later with thankfulness.

Serving

We have looked briefly at the importance of saving during your youth. Saving is critical because it becomes much more difficult to do after marriage. But this same principle is also true with regard to serving others. You will find much less available time to help others when you have a family to take care of.

You are living in a world of need. There are critical needs on a global level, needs in your community, and needs right in your local congregation. As you grow in maturity and the Lord helps you take your eyes off your own desires, you will see even more of the needs that surround you. But unfortunately, about the time we "grow up" and begin to see the needs more clearly, we no longer have the time to help as we would like.

I have watched this cycle. A young teenage girl lives a carefree life, with her parents providing for her needs. She focuses on social functions, peer pressures, and how she fits in with her friends, and then she marries. As children begin to come and life becomes more hectic, she becomes more aware of the burdens of life. In the middle of the daily grind, she longs for someone who could just stop in and bake some cookies or help with the cleaning. But the young girls in her congregation seem preoccupied with their social lives. They don't seem to notice the young mothers who are surrounded by mountains of dirty laundry, have several children crying for attention, and are trying to stay ahead of the garden and bills.

Then this young mother's mind goes back. She thinks about all of the time she wasted when she was young. How many days did she lose while preoccupied with acceptance by peers? How many young mothers could she have helped during those years?

You have an amazing opportunity to serve in your youth. If your heart is open to living for the Lord, it can be a wonderful time to bless others, whether within your own community or in destitute parts of the world. Either way, you will never regret time spent serving others. These times will provide a point of reference that will bless you the rest of your life. If you are able to help in a foreign setting, you will have a different perspective on how much wealth is needed to be content. If you are able to live for a while in different homes, it will give you an education and a broader point of view on child training techniques. I would encourage you to use this time of your life to serve. It is a brief and valuable opportunity for the young man or woman wise enough to use it.

Conclusion

While many today look back with regret, I have also listened to young people who can reflect with joy. They have used this time of their lives to properly plan for the future and to bless others. We are young only once. Society will tell you to get all the fun out of this period that you possibly can. Our world will encourage you to do whatever feels good and provides the greatest thrill. But God is asking you to walk away from the call of the world. He wants you to openly commit to serving Him. It is a wonderful time, and I believe you will look back on these years with great joy and satisfaction if your time is spent saving and serving!

For Further Reflection

1. Share some experiences you have had in serving others. How have you been blessed by those experiences? In what ways has your life been changed?

2. Discuss the difference between saving and hoarding. As a young man saves for the future, how can he avoid hoarding?

3. Discuss some blessings of serving at home. Why do we tend to find serving away from home more enjoyable?

4. The two times in life that most people have extra time and money is when they are young and when they are old. Share your vision for your older years. How do you want your extra time and money to be used during those years? How can you prepare for that time now?

Materialism—Satan's Sneaky Substitute | 24

THE CARES OF THIS WORLD, AND THE DECEITFULNESS OF RICHES, AND THE LUSTS OF OTHER THINGS ENTERING IN, CHOKE THE WORD, AND IT BECOMETH UNFRUITFUL.

MARK 4:19

In 1682 John Bunyan published a book that attempts to portray the battle that goes on within the mind and the importance of defensive warfare in the life of a believer. This book, *Holy War*, has never been as popular as *Pilgrim's Progress*, but it does present a vivid illustration. He portrays the mind as a city—the city of Mansoul. Mansoul has five gates, and each gate represents one of our natural senses—sight, touch, smell, taste, and hearing. Passage through these gates is the only hope the enemy has of victory, so the gates become the battle sites. Throughout the book, Diabolus (representing Satan) tries different strategies to penetrate the gates and persuade the city to let him be king. At times the citizens of Mansoul choose to have Shaddai (representing God) as king, at other times Diabolus. But toward the end of the book, after Diabolus has repeatedly attacked with violence, tried various attempts at deception, and fought many bloody battles, a demon called Legion presents a plan we should take note of.

Legion proposes an entirely different strategy. Instead of threats, insults, and violence, Legion suggests they start blessing the people materially. "Stuff them with goods!" he suggests. "They'll be forced to make their castle a warehouse instead of a garrison fortified against us!"[1]

Instead of fighting them at the gates and along the walls of the city, Legion suggested they take the battle to the marketplace. Give them so much stuff to enjoy that they forget the battle. Feed them anything they desire, and they will grow sleepy and apathetic. In short, Legion was proposing they use the weapon of materialism. Instead of trying to persuade the people to serve Satan, they would provide a sneaky, subtle substitute. Satan is the master of substitutes. If he can't win with direct confrontation, he'll try an alternative.

Possessions, Money, and the Early Church

Let's go back for a minute and look at how the church began. How did early Christians regard wealth and possessions? It is evident that the church in the book of Acts gave some thought to the subject. In fact, one of the first things they did following conversion was deal with their finances. The account says that they "sold their possessions and goods, and parted them to all men, as every man had need."[a]

One of the very first things they did as new believers was to deal with their money and possessions. It appears this was the immediate response to the infilling of the Spirit and their desire to be like Jesus. A little later we see Satan harassing those new converts. It was the first wave of persecution, and the disciples cried out to God for direction and power. The Bible says that as they prayed, the place where they were gathered was shaken, and they were all filled with the Holy Ghost. But notice again the immediate result of the Spirit of God upon their lives. "And the multitude of them that believed were of one heart and of one soul: neither said any of them that ought of the things which he possessed was his own; but they had all things common."[b]

Again, as the Spirit of God worked within their hearts, it affected their possessions and wealth. Recently I was reading a modern writing regarding this account, and the writer said he believed the disciples got a little carried away here. He said that in their enthusiasm they went beyond what was really necessary. But I wonder. Does the church in America possess the same strength those early believers had? Are we seeing the same spirit and zeal that they experienced? Is there a connection between vitality in the church and how we deal with our possessions and money?

Those early believers endured persecution for several hundred years, and then suddenly peace came. In 313 A.D., the emperor Constantine issued the Edict of Milan, which allowed his subjects to worship any

[a]Acts 2:45
[b]Acts 4:32

god they wished. But he did more than just that. Christianity was the religion of the emperor himself, and he used public money to build elaborate churches. He began to pay the church leaders so they could devote more of their time to praying and blessing their congregations.

Persecution to Prosperity

We cannot comprehend the sudden change the church experienced. Imagine going from being hunted, imprisoned, and horribly tortured to suddenly being paid and honored just for being a leader in the church. We can hardly blame Christians for being swept off their feet after suffering violent persecution for hundreds of years. It would have been hard to believe this sudden ease and prosperity was not from God Himself. But as their view toward wealth, ease, and separation from the world changed, something else changed too.

AS THEIR VIEW TOWARD WEALTH, EASE, AND SEPARATION FROM THE WORLD CHANGED, SOMETHING ELSE CHANGED TOO. THEY LOST THEIR POWER.

They lost their power. No longer did their neighbors see them as different. The church was chasing after the same things the world was chasing. The world viewed the accumulation of wealth and possessions as important, and so did the church. Its light had gone out. Secular history refers to the years that followed as the Dark Ages.

We look back over that period of time with regret. If only the early church could have preserved its initial fire. What would have happened if Christians had retained their original view of earthly possessions? What could the church have been like if they had continued to view the accumulation of wealth as a snare—something that gets in the way of devotion to Christ and His Kingdom? We may never know, but we should be asking ourselves even more pressing questions.

What could the church be like today if we had the same regard for wealth and possessions that those early believers had? What kind of revival could break out in America if our neighbors could see by our choices that we have no regard for the materialism that surrounds us? What if those we work with every day saw people with such a passion for the Kingdom that they were totally oblivious to the cheap tinsel and glitter around them?

From Power to Pies

It is imperative that we understand where we are in history. Many of us have ancestors who were persecuted and imprisoned for their faith in the sixteenth and seventeenth centuries. Many of them were burned at the stake, drowned in rivers, and boiled in pots of oil. They spent their years in hiding, fleeing religious persecution. But all that is over now. Now the Anabaptist movement is known not for passion for the Kingdom, but for large farms and delicious pies. Tour buses weave through many communities so tourists can get a glimpse of these quaint people. We are known for loving our culture rather than loving the Kingdom.

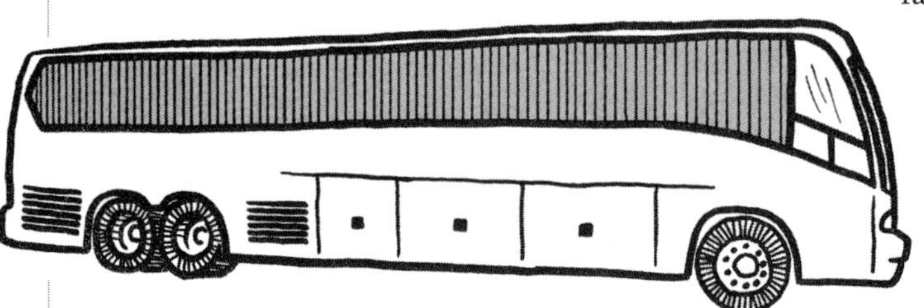

Things are much clearer in history. We look back on those believers during the time of Constantine and wish we could wake them up. "Can't you see what is happening?" we feel like shouting. "Don't you see that you are giving up God's best for a little earthly pleasure?" Couldn't those early believers under Constantine see what Satan was doing? Just a little ease and comfort, and they were knocked right off their feet.

But I wonder what our time would look like if we could move forward a few hundred years and look back. What if we could compare the power those early Anabaptists experienced with the deadness we experience in our lives and churches today? If time lasts and our descendants are able to read the history of our time, what do you suppose they will say? I wonder if they might also have a desire to call back to us, "Can't you see what Satan is doing? Don't you see how he has turned your affection from simplicity in Christ to a love for the world? Don't you understand why your neighbors are no longer interested in what you have to offer? Your love of the world and pursuit of materialism are confusing the very people God is trying to reach!"

Clearly, Satan is going after your generation with a vengeance. Every age has had its challenges, but I believe young believers today are in a battle more intense than any previous generation. Satan knows his time is short, and he is pulling out all the stops. He is attacking in more areas than just materialism. We could talk about morality, music, dress, and respect for authority. But as we continue to focus on materialism, let's look at a couple of Satan's subtle tactics.

Gluttony and Global Reality

Several years ago I walked onto a construction site and overheard two young men talking. One of them had gone out to eat the night before at a local steakhouse, and he was telling the other about his experience.

"It was awesome," he said. "The food was great, and it's really a nice place."

The other man turned and asked with interest, "So how much did it cost?"

"Oh, it was about twenty dollars a plate," he replied. "But it was worth it. The food was really good!"

That brief discussion replayed in my mind for several days. "Twenty dollars a plate, but it was worth it." How do you decide whether something is "worth it" or not? I pictured many of the conditions in the world and what twenty dollars could do. Medical clinics turn people away due to lack of funds. Believers go without Bibles due to lack of resources. More than fifteen people die from hunger every minute, and 75 percent of those are children.[2] Is a twenty-dollar steak worth it? In the middle of this

> IS A TWENTY-DOLLAR STEAK WORTH IT?

overfed, overindulgent, and overweight culture, do we even know the value of twenty dollars?

Those two young men were not selfish or uninterested in helping. They had just been shielded from global reality. I believe God is calling your generation to self-denial in ways that perhaps your parents have not considered. Paul told the church at Galatia, "As we have therefore opportunity, let us do good unto all men, especially unto them who are of the household of faith."[c]

There has never been a generation with more opportunity. Youth today have been given tremendous resources, and with those resources comes responsibility. You can heap these resources upon yourself, or you can choose to build the Kingdom of God by being a channel for those resources to bless those in need. The choice is before you.

Stuff and Storage

Let's look for a moment at the world you have inherited. You have been born into a society that continues to chase after more and more. Consider the size of houses. In the early 1940s the average house in America was around 750 square feet. During the fifties the average climbed to 950 square feet, and in the sixties the average rose to about 1,100. This means that the average house in America grew almost 50 percent in about twenty years.

In the seventies new houses being built were up to an average of 1,350 square feet, and if your family is average, the house your parents raised you in was probably over 2,300 square feet.[3] Keep in mind that during those years the average family size was actually shrinking.

But the amazing part of this is that the average American living in these large houses feels constricted. The closets are full, the car is in the driveway because the garage is full, and many people have more stuff in a storage facility in town. Storage has become a major industry in America. In fact, Americans spend over twenty billion dollars every year just storing their stuff. Statistics show that nearly one in every eleven homes rents a self-storage unit.[4]

Or consider this. If you could put all the storage units in the United

[c]Galatians 6:10

States together, they would cover about seventy-eight square miles! That is about seven square feet for every man, woman, and child in the United States. Satan's strategy is no longer a secret; it should be obvious![5] Many of us are groaning under the weight of all this stuff. Just think about the ways this affluence saps our resources. We find a gadget that intrigues us. We pay for the product, spend time and money maintaining the thing, focus on protecting it, eventually pay someone to store it, and finally pay the landfill to dispose of it.

God is calling your generation back to a life of separation and simplicity. For too long we have followed the world in this cycle of consumerism. As Christmas approaches, we feel pressured, and we strain our brains to think of something Uncle Henry doesn't have. In desperation, we finally settle on another gadget Uncle Henry didn't know he wanted and in fact may not have known existed. Uncle Henry enjoys the gadget, but after a while loses interest, and the trinket disappears into the closet. It will stay there until the closet is full, when it will be transferred to the garage, and then on to the storage unit in town.

But I have been encouraged by listening to discussions among many of our youth. Youth are waking up to global reality. We need to keep gathering with our families during special times of the year, but could we think of better ways to use our resources than buying unneeded items? Recently I have heard of several families who, instead of giving each other gifts, gave to charities and then told the family members where the money went. One individual mentioned that his mother did this last year, and the card he received from the organization was his best Christmas present ever. In the midst of a society that seems to be breathlessly chasing just one more gadget, could you demonstrate something different? Yes, continue caring for and focusing on your parents and siblings, but I wonder if they don't need your time more than your trinkets. I wonder how our families and churches would be affected if we spent less time in the mall and more time together discussing topics that really matter.

Recommitment to the Kingdom

It has been over three hundred years since John Bunyan wrote the book *Holy War*, and there is no way he could have predicted the materialistic climate we find ourselves in today. Yet it seems clear we are living in the exact scenario Bunyan depicted in his account. The god of this world is flooding our lives with goods and stuff. Materialism is stealing our resources, our time, and our thought life. It is time for the church to confess that we have given ground in this area and renounce the god of this world.

But deciding not to buy more stuff is only half of the equation. We can live very frugal lives and still be of no value to our Lord. There is no value in poverty without purpose. Our real need is recommitment to the Kingdom. Jesus is calling us to be His hands and feet and accomplish His work here on earth. We are to use His resources for His purpose.

> THERE IS NO VALUE IN POVERTY WITHOUT PURPOSE.

Sometimes we speak of Sodom and Gomorrah, and we think of them as so immoral that God finally destroyed them. In fact, even today we refer to extreme immorality as sodomy. But was this all that God was angry about? Notice what the prophet Ezekiel said about the sin of Sodom: "Behold, this was the iniquity of thy sister Sodom, pride, fulness of bread, and abundance of idleness was in her and in her daughters, neither did she strengthen the hand of the poor and needy."[d]

As God views the world today, I wonder what He would say about us. I wonder how far we are from the sin of Sodom. How does He view our lives? Is our way of living really different from the world's? Or are we neglecting God's best and finding satisfaction in materialism, Satan's sneaky substitute?

Conclusion

I don't know what your experience has been or how far you have come in your Christian walk. I don't know how you have used your time and money in the past or how Satan is tempting you today. Your generation is facing challenges your parents knew nothing of. But I

[d]Ezekiel 16:49

want to encourage you to follow Jesus regardless. Let His teachings and simplicity of lifestyle be a pattern for your life.

It is an exciting time to be alive, and today's opportunities exceed anything previous generations have known. Each generation becomes known for something, and my prayer is that yours will become famous as well. Not for your possessions, your prosperity, or your pies, but for using the amazing opportunities and financial resources you have been given to build the Kingdom of Jesus Christ.

For Further Reflection

1. Make five lists, one for each of our senses. Under each sense, write down materialistic temptations Satan uses to lure us away from a Kingdom focus.

2. Can you share a time when you couldn't think of anything to give someone at Christmas? What are some other ways this season could be celebrated by your family?

3. Is there a connection between our lack of spiritual vitality and how we view our money and possessions? Share why you think there is or isn't.

4. Imagine you are living one hundred years from now. Write down what you think you would say about this current generation.

5. As you conclude this study, name some areas where you have been personally challenged. Share any resolves you have made in your own life in the area of financial stewardship.

Endnotes

INTRODUCTION

[1]Thieleman J. van Braght, *Martyrs Mirror*, Herald Press, 1997, p. 256, <http://www.homecomers.org/mirror/martyrs034.htm>, accessed on April 18, 2010.

CHAPTER Seven

[1]Fred Moore, "The Gospel Outreach Story," <http://goaim.org/about-us/the-gospel-outreach-story/>, accessed on March 2, 2010.
[2]"Count Your Blessings," <http://www.iciworld.net/articles/countyourblessings.htm>, accessed on March 2, 2010.
[3]Wade Horn and Andrew Bush, *Fathers, Marriage, and Welfare Reform*, Hudson Institute, Indianapolis, 1997, quoted by Larry Bilotta, <www.marriage-success-secrets.com/statistics-about-children-and-divorce.html>, accessed March 5, 2010.

CHAPTER ELEVEN

[1]Jeffery G. MacDonald, "On A Mission—A Short-Term Mission," *USA Today*, June 18, 2006.

CHAPTER THIRTEEN

[1]Gary Miller, *Budgeting Made Simple*, TGS International, Berlin, OH, 2010.

CHAPTER FOURTEEN

[1]Thomas L. Friedman, *The World Is Flat*, Penguin Books, London, 2005.
[2]Ibid., p. 13.

CHAPTER SEVENTEEN

[1]Randy Alcorn, *Money, Possessions, and Eternity*, Tyndale House Publishers, Wheaton, Illinois, 1989, p. 207.

CHAPTER EIGHTEEN

[1]The University of Washington, Washington State Department of Health

and Washington State ECEAP, *ClicKit! To Reduce Television in Early Childhood*, p. 8.
[2]Katie Hafner, "Texting May Be Taking a Toll," *The New York Times*, (New York Edition) May 25, 2009, Sec. D, p.1.
[3]Kaiser Family Foundation, "Daily Media Use Among Children and Teens Up Dramatically From Five Years Ago," January 20, 2010, <http://www.kff.org/entmedia/entmedia012010nr.cfm>, accessed on April 10, 2010.

Chapter Twenty-Two

[1]Nancy Castleman, "Upfront Reward Visa Platinum: There's Never Been a Credit Card Like It," November 3, 2006, <http://www.credit.com/blog/2006/11/theres_never_be/>, accessed on May 19, 2010.
[2]Liz Pulliam Weston, MSN Money, quoted in "Credit Card Act Raises Debate," The University of Northern Iowa Student Newspaper, March 8, 2010, <http://www.northern-iowan.org/credit-card-act-raises-debate-1.2183827>, accessed on May 19, 2010.
[3]Lisa Beach, "Should Teens Have Credit Cards?" October 19, 2008, <http://www.helium.com/items/1210430-teens-and-credit-cards-teen-credit-debt-teens-and-money>, accessed on May 20, 2010.
[4]IndexCreditCards, <http://www.indexcreditcards.com/creditcardnews/credit-card-terms-your-agreement-online/>, accessed on May 20, 2010.
[5]Seeking Alpha, "Guide to Credit Cards; How Credit Cards Encourage You to Overspend," November 3, 2006, <http://seekingalpha.com/article/20333-guide-to-credit-cards-how-credit-cards-encourage-you-to-overspend>, accessed on May 20, 2010.
[6]Art Markman, Ph.D., "Ulterior Motives," *Psychology Today*, January 26, 2010, <http://www.psychologytoday.com/blog/ulterior-motives/201001/spending-and-credit-cards>, accessed on May 22, 2010.
[7]Howard Rachlin, *The Science of Self-Control*, Harvard University Press, Cambridge, Massachusetts, 2002, p. 39.

Chapter Twenty-Four

[1]John Bunyan (as told by Ethel Barrett), *The War for Mansoul* (abridged rendition of *Holy War)*, Christian Light Publications, Harrisonburg, Virginia, 1998, p. 166.
[2]Anup Shah, "Today Over 22,000 Children Died Around the World," <http://www.globalissues.org/article/715/today-over-22000-children-died-around-the-world>, accessed on May 25, 2010.
[3]John de Graaf, David Wann, and Thomas Naylor, *Affluenza*, Berrett-Koehler Publishers, Inc., San Francisco, 2001, p. 24.
[4]Joshua Becker, "The Statistics of Clutter," <http://www.becomingminimalist.com/2010/01/19/the-statistics-of-clutter/>, accessed May 27, 2010.
[5]James A. Bacon, "The Excesses of Affluence," May 28, 2007, <http://www.baconsrebellion.com/Issues07/05-28/Bacon.php>, accessed on May 28, 2010.

About the Author

Gary Miller was raised in an Anabaptist community in California and today lives with his wife Patty and family in the Pacific Northwest. Gary's desire has been to encourage Christians in developed countries to share their resources and focus more on the Kingdom of God. He also continues to work with the poor in Third World countries and manages the SALT Microfinance Solutions program for Christian Aid Ministries.

Gary's enthusiasm for Kingdom building has prompted him to share his vision in writing. Seeing a need for Christians in all age groups to take a fresh look at their goals and priorities in life, especially in finances, Gary began to develop the Kingdom-Focused Living series. His first book in the series, *Kingdom-Focused Finances,* was released in 2010.

If you have comments about any of the Kingdom-Focused Living books, you can share your thoughts by sending an e-mail to kingdomfinance@camoh.org or writing to Christian Aid Ministries, P.O. Box 360, Berlin, Ohio, 44610.

Additional books by Gary Miller

PUBLISHED BY CHRISTIAN AID MINISTRIES

Kingdom-Focused Finances for the Family

This first book in the Kingdom-Focused Living series is realistic, humorous, and serious about getting us to become stewards instead of owners.

Going Till You're Gone

A plea for godly examples—for older men and women who will demonstrate a Kingdom-focused vision all the way to the finish line.

Budgeting Made Simple

A budgeting workbook in a ring binder; complements *Kingdom-Focused Finances for the Family.*

Small Business Handbook

A manual used in microfinance programs in Third World countries. Includes devotionals and practical business teaching. Ideal for missions and churches.

Haiti Earthquake: Heartache and Hope

Filled with full-color photos and heart-wrenching, firsthand accounts of relief workers and victims, this book tells the story of the mind-boggling destruction and death in Haiti from the earthquake of January 12, 2010.

AUDIO BOOKS, NARRATED BY THE AUTHOR

Kingdom-Focused Finances for the Family, Charting A Course in Your Youth, and *Going Till You're Gone.*

AUDIO AND POWER POINT SEMINARS

Kingdom-Focused Finances Seminar—3 audio CDs

This three-session seminar takes you beyond our culture's view of money and possessions, and challenges you to examine your heart by looking at your treasure.

Kingdom-Focused Finances Seminar Audio Power Point—3 CDs

With the visual aid included on these CDs, you can now follow along on the slides Gary uses in his seminars while you listen to the presentation. A good tool for group study or individual use. A computer is needed to view these CDs.

Christian Aid Ministries

Christian Aid Ministries was founded in 1981 as a nonprofit, tax-exempt 501(c)(3) organization. Its primary purpose is to provide a trustworthy and efficient channel for Amish, Mennonite, and other conservative Anabaptist groups and individuals to minister to physical and spiritual needs around the world. This is in response to the command ". . . do good unto all men, especially unto them who are of the household of faith" (Gal. 6:10).

Each year, CAM supporters provide approximately 15 million pounds of food, clothing, medicines, seeds, Bibles, Bible story books, and other Christian literature for needy people. Most of the aid goes to orphans and Christian families. Supporters' funds also help clean up and rebuild for natural disaster victims, put up Gospel billboards in the U.S., support several church-planting efforts, operate two medical clinics, and provide resources for needy families to make their own living. CAM's main purposes for providing aid are to help and encourage God's people and bring the Gospel to a lost and dying world.

CAM has staff, warehouse, and distribution networks in Romania, Moldova, Ukraine, Haiti, Nicaragua, Liberia, and Israel. Aside from management, supervisory personnel, and bookkeeping operations, volunteers do most of the work at CAM locations. Each year, volunteers at our warehouses, field bases, DRS projects, and other locations donate over 200,000 hours of work.

CAM's ultimate purpose is to glorify God and help enlarge His kingdom. ". . . whatsoever ye do, do all to the glory of God" (I Cor. 10:31).

The Way to God and Peace

We live in a world contaminated by sin. Sin is anything that goes against God's holy standards. When we do not follow the guidelines that God our Creator gave us, we are guilty of sin. Sin separates us from God, the source of life.

Since the time when the first man and woman, Adam and Eve, sinned in the Garden of Eden, sin has been universal. The Bible says that we all have "sinned and come short of the glory of God" (Romans 3:23). It also says that the natural consequence for that sin is eternal death, or punishment in an eternal hell: "Then when lust hath conceived, it bringeth forth sin: and sin, when it is finished, bringeth forth death" (James 1:15).

But we do not have to suffer eternal death in hell. God provided forgiveness for our sins through the death of His only Son, Jesus Christ. Because Jesus was perfect and without sin, He could die in our place. "For God so loved the world that he gave his only begotten Son, that whosoever believeth in him should not perish, but have everlasting life" (John 3:16).

A sacrifice is something given to benefit someone else. It costs the giver greatly. Jesus was God's sacrifice. Jesus' death takes away the penalty of sin for everyone who accepts this sacrifice and truly repents of their sins. To repent of sins means to be truly sorry for and turn away from the things we have done that have violated God's standards. (Acts 2:38; 3:19).

Jesus died, but He did not remain dead. After three days, God's Spirit miraculously raised Him to life again. God's Spirit does something similar in us. When we receive Jesus as our sacrifice and repent of our sins, our hearts are changed. We become spiritually alive! We develop new desires and attitudes (2 Corinthians 5:17). We begin to make choices that please God (1 John 3:9). If we do fail and commit sins, we can ask God for forgiveness. "If we confess our sins, he is faithful and just to forgive us our sins, and to cleanse us from all unrighteousness" (1 John 1:9).

Once our hearts have been changed, we want to continue growing spiritually. We will be happy to let Jesus be the Master of our lives and will want to become more like Him. To do this, we must meditate on God's Word and commune with God in prayer. We will testify to others of this change by being baptized and sharing the good news of God's victory over sin and death. Fellowship with a faithful group of believers will strengthen our walk with God (1 John 1:7).